BLITZ SPIRIT

BLITZ SPIRIT

BRAVERY PATRIOTISM HUMOUR

Compiled by

Jaqueline Mitchell

Bounty
Books

First published in Great Britain in 2010 by Osprey Publishing Ltd

This edition published in 2011 by Bounty Books,
by arrangement with Osprey Publishing Ltd

Bounty Books is a division of Octopus Publishing Group Ltd
Endeavour House
189 Shaftesbury Avenue
London WC2H 8JY

www.octopusbooks.co.uk

An Hachette UK Company
www.hachette.co.uk

Introduction, selection and compilation © Jaqueline Mitchell 2010

ISBN: 978-0-753722-36-7

Page layout by Myriam Bell Design, France
Typeset in Cochin and Bernard Condensed

A CIP catalogue record for this book is available from
the British Library

Printed and bound in China

Imperial War Museum Collections

Many of the photos in this book come from the Imperial War Museum's huge collections which cover
all aspects of conflict involving Britain and the Commonwealth since the start of the twentieth century.
These rich resources are available online to search, browse and buy at www.iwmcollections.org.uk. In
addition to Collections Online, you can visit the Visitor Rooms where you can explore over 8 million
photographs, thousands of hours of moving images, the largest sound archive of its kind in the world,
thousands of diaries and letters written by people in wartime, and a huge reference library.
To make an appointment visit http://www.iwm.org.uk/

CONTENTS

INTRODUCTION

One cold, snowy evening in February 1941, my grandfather went to the Swansea Empire to enjoy the variety show. Shortly after 7.30pm bombs began to fall on the quiet streets, and when he left they were in darkness, the sirens having sounded as bombs descended on the town, targeting the docks. There were no buses, and so he was compelled to walk the few miles from the town centre back home to Sketty. Each time he heard the screaming of the bombs he dived for cover into the bushes at the side of the road. In the meantime, his wife and daughter hid under the stairs. All survived.

Up the road, my grandmother's hairdresser, and her family, were invited to join their neighbours in an Anderson Shelter. She was a large woman, and after some time could stand the claustrophobic atmosphere no longer. She went back home. The shelter received a direct hit and was flattened; she had a made a lucky escape.

The experience for the people during this dark period in Britain's history was very frightening. For years afterwards, whenever my mother heard aeroplanes overhead, her heart would flutter. Many thought that the country was in danger of invasion, fortifications were built along the coast and barrage balloons floated overhead.

For Swansea, this was the first of three nights of bombing; 7,000 lost their homes and 230 people were killed. Hitler's *Blitzkrieg* on Britain had begun on 7 September 1940, when at around 5pm German bombers were spotted coming towards London. The bombing continued for hours until dawn, and that first night 437 civilians died, 1,600 more being seriously injured and thousands losing their homes. Ack-ack guns responded but they were largely ineffective. Two days later, on 9 September, the King visited the East End, where whole terraces of houses had been destroyed. On Friday 13th Buckingham Palace itself was attacked, two bombs falling nearby and others crashing into the quadrangle and damaging the chapel. Famously, the Queen remarked, 'I'm glad we've been bombed. It makes me feel I can look the East End in the face.'

This was the start of the Blitz. For 76 nights the raids continued on London, shattering the inhabitants' nerves, and causing children to be evacuated to safety. Initially aimed at London, other cities would also suffer: Coventry, Belfast, Birmingham, Bristol, Swansea, Manchester, Hull, Liverpool, Plymouth, Southampton, Clydebank among them. 'The Front is everywhere' wrote Vera Brittain in the introduction to *England's Hour*, published in February 1941. 'In addition to capital cities, all the towns, villages and hamlets of every combatant country are potential battlefields.' By the time the persistent bombing came to an end in May 1941 – when Hitler turned his attention to the Eastern Front – over 30,000 Britons had been killed and nearly two and a half times that number injured. Around 2 million houses had been damaged or destroyed, 60 per cent in the capital.

On 6 September 1940, Noel Coward, then in America, wrote to his confidante and secretary Lorn Loraine, how the 'performance of the Air Force and the people of England generally, is having a tremendous effect on the people over here. I get into awful states now and then when I read of the bombings and wish I was there with you all very much indeed. Sometimes being so far away is almost more than I can bear.' The following year, his home in Gerald Road was damaged. While it was being repaired, he went to Wales, where he wrote *Blithe Spirit* – one of the most successful shows of the wartime period, it opened in July 1941. It is Coward's wartime songs, most memorably perhaps 'London Pride', that capture the undaunted spirit of his fellow Londoners. Dance halls continued to fill, while new songs and dances such as the jitterbug and the 'Black-out Stroll' gained immediate popularity.

People built Anderson Shelters in their gardens – looking like large old-fashioned pigsties, with corrugated metal roofs, these were dug into the ground, and intended to provide shelter from the worst of the bombs. For those who did not have a garden, Morrison shelters were available. Black-outs, to hide location from the Germans, became customary, and a plethora of books were published to provide home-made entertainment to while away the long nights. In London thousands found shelter in the Underground (the sight of them movingly recorded by artists Henry Moore, Edward Ardizzone and Olga Lehmann); crammed together, they brought sandwiches, toys and small home comforts with them. A pragmatic improvisation took hold: at the Ritz Hotel in London, cooking was done on upended electric radiators during power cuts, and it was a case of make do and mend elsewhere.

The Ministry of Information went into overdrive, producing films, leaflets, posters and other materials, including cigarette

What do I do...

with these "What do I do" announcements?

I read them carefully wherever I see them, because they contain *official* information in a short form on the subjects they deal with.

I cut them out and keep them, because today's subject may be an answer for tomorrow's problem.

I see to it that my family read them too. "I never knew" is no excuse today!

Cut this out—and keep it!

*Issued by the Ministry of Information
Space presented to the Nation
by the Brewers' Society*

cards produced with the tobacco manufacturer W.D. and H.G. Wills (now part of Imperial Tobacco Company), advising people on air raid precautions. James A. Milne was among those to produce guides for the many volunteers – his *Fitness in Defence* was aimed at 'the Home Guard, National Fire Service, Air Raid Wardens, War Reserve Constabulary, Air Training Corps, the Boy Scouts, the workers, the people'. On the radio, which then commanded many millions of listeners, J.B. Priestley was commissioned to make broadcasts explaining events, in an attempt to bring solace and boost morale. His audience, according to Angus Calder (in *The Myth of the Blitz*), averaged 31 per cent of the nation. Mollie Panter-Downes, an Englishwoman, sent a letter fortnightly to *The New Yorker*, keeping those Stateside informed.

Despite the discomfort, despite the hardship, despite the fear, the British came through. The Home Guard (the renamed Local Defence Volunteers) was formed to defend Britain in case of invasion, and ARP wardens ensured that the strictures of the black-out were obeyed. Thousands in cities and towns throughout Britain signed up to help the country in its 'finest hour': to man mobile canteens or ambulances, to be ARP wardens or join the Home Guard, to join the WVS or help in the hospitals, to knit and write to the 'boys' overseas, and to be part of the Mass Observation corps that would report on wartime in Britain (some of whose accounts are included here). Many were the anonymous unsung heroes. Young fireman F.W. Hurd commended the Watchroom staffs in the control room during the big raids on the East End in London in September 1940: 'They are the people to thank for getting fires attended as soon as they break out', he commented, 'hard at it, often all night, under pretty tough conditions.' By the year's end he himself would be dead, killed during a raid on 29/30 December.

Within this book is a compilation of precautionary advice and warning posters issued by the Home Office and the Ministry of Information, extracts from the training manual of the Home Guard, first-hand accounts which bring home the fear and also the quiet courage and determination that largely held out despite the destruction and dismay, some of the songs and poems written at the time to cheer and charm, the rousing speeches which Churchill made to the nation, which both brought a sense of unity and lifted morale, and photographs which depict, in sometimes horrifying, graphic detail, the current of daily lives during the Blitz. Included too are extracts which display flashes of the, sometimes black, British humour which rose to make fun of things in Britain's bleakest and, according to Churchill, also its 'finest' hour. Arranged in more or less chronological order, they tell the story of the Blitz.

Crowds gather at the Elephant and Castle tube station.

When it was all over, when the troops returned, many found their homes battered, if not broken. It would be over fifty years, on 29 December 2006, before Britain finally repaid America the monies given it under the Lend-Lease programme, funds vital for its continuing effort. Rationing would continue until 1954. And the world had changed. But it had been a world worth fighting for and, in time, Britain's people would find their way back to the ordinary, domestic, family lives they had so missed and craved. And the majority of us, those generations descended from them – their children and grandchildren and great-grandchildren – have reason to be forever grateful to them.

'WE SHALL NEVER SURRENDER'

Winston Churchill

I have, myself, full confidence that if all do their duty, if nothing is neglected, and if the best arrangements are made, as they are being made, we shall prove ourselves once again able to defend our island home, to ride out the storm of war, and to outlive the menace of tyranny, if necessary for years, if necessary alone. At any rate, that is what we are going to try to do. That is the resolve of His Majesty's Government – every man of them. That is the will of Parliament and the nation. [...] Even though large tracts of Europe and many old and famous States have fallen or may fall into the grip of the Gestapo and all the odious apparatus of Nazi rule, we shall not flag or fail. We shall go on to the end. We shall fight in France, we shall fight on the seas and oceans, we shall fight with growing confidence and growing strength in the air, we shall defend our island, whatever the cost may be. We shall fight on the beaches, we shall fight on the landing grounds, we shall fight in the fields and in the streets, we shall fight in the hills; we shall never surrender...

4 June 1940

Winston Churchill inspects a Thompson sub-machine gun.

THE 'FOURTH DEFENCE SERVICE'

The object of enemy air raids is to dislocate the war effort of the nation. The attainment of this object may be sought by deliberate attacks on targets of military significance, a term having a wide application in these days, or by unrestricted and indiscriminate bombing of the civil population. The primary responsibility for resisting the enemy's efforts lies with the active defence services. But it is essential to have available a nationwide organization, the purpose of which is to minimize the effects of air raids which might occur as a result of the enemy being successful in penetrating the active defences. Such an organization has been built up and forms what might now be referred to as the Fourth Defence Service. The operation of this service is the responsibility of local authorities in the United Kingdom, working under the general direction of the Ministry of Home Security.

THE WARNING SYSTEM

A means by which warning can be given to the general public of an approaching raid is of first importance, and this is provided by a national system. Warning messages are sent out to the districts where air attack may materialize. In those districts only is the 'Action Warning' sounded by sirens, and the signal is a 'warbling' note given on a variable pitch siren, or a succession of 5-second blasts sounded on a fixed-pitch hooter followed by intervals of 3 seconds. The warning is then taken up locally by sharp blasts on police and wardens' whistles.

When the raid has passed or is no longer expected, this is announced by a continuous blast sounded upon any type of siren. This signal is known as 'Raiders Passed'. All siren signals are sounded for a period of two minutes.

If the presence of gas is suspected, warning of it is given locally by wardens' hand rattles; and when the area is known to be safe again this warning is cancelled by the ringing of wardens' handbells, which announces the 'All Clear'.

AIR RAID WARDENS

There will be a great need in time of air raids for persons of courage and personality, with a sound knowledge of the locality, to advise and help their neighbours, and generally to serve as a link between the public and the authorities. To provide for this, the Air Raid Wardens Service has been organized and is based topographically on Sectors and Posts under a Chief Warden in

AIR RAID PRECAUTIONS BADGE

each local area. In the London Region, areas of Wardens' Posts are grouped as Districts under District Wardens.

Wardens have important duties to carry out, including assessing air raid damage, reporting it concisely and correctly, guiding and assisting the ARP services sent to deal with it, and giving general assistance and guidance to members of the public. Their functions are in some respects allied to those of the police, with whom they will need to co-operate closely; and, though they are not part of the police or special constabulary, the wardens' service is generally placed by the local authority under the executive control of the Chief Constable.

AUXILIARY FIRE SERVICE

It is important that fires should be tackled at their inception, as they are more easily extinguished at this stage than later. Incendiary bombs may cause fires in such large numbers in a comparatively restricted area that the normal resources of the Fire Brigade will be inadequate. An Auxiliary Fire Service has therefore been formed. Specially designed equipment is supplied to this service; this normally takes the form of trailer pumps, drawn by cars, taxis, and vans, but self-propelled units and fire-floats are supplied in appropriate cases.

DECONTAMINATION SQUADS

Areas where persistent gas has fallen are said to be contaminated, and are dangerous until the gas has been neutralized or removed. The work of decontamination is related generally to that of the Street Cleansing Services, and special Decontamination Squads, consisting of a foreman and five men with the addition of a driver, have been recruited, principally from these services, for the work.

GAS IDENTIFICATION SERVICE

If poison gas is used, wardens will immediately report the fact. They will also warn the public. There may arise problems in connection with gas warfare, however, which require the services of experts, and to provide for this a local Gas Identification Service, consisting of specially trained chemists, has been formed and equipped with apparatus suitable for their specialized duties.

FIRST AID PARTIES

There may be injured who must be given attention where they lie; some will require removal for further treatment. For this work there are First Aid (or Stretcher) Parties, each consisting of four men with a driver and transport for themselves and vehicles for the injured provided by the Ambulance Service.

FIRST AID POSTS AND HOSPITALS

There must be places where the lightly and seriously injured can be treated, and this is done at First Aid Posts and Hospitals. First Aid Posts are normally in buildings adapted and equipped for this work. They are supplemented by Mobile Units, consisting of vehicles in which the appropriate equipment and staff are conveyed to scenes of damage in order that temporary First Aid Posts may be established near by.

In rural districts First Aid Points are established, and consist of a first aid box placed in some central building where attention to the injured can be given.

RESCUE PARTIES

Those who have been trapped in shelters or under buildings must be released. This work requires experience and care, since debris unskilfully moved might release other parts of the structure, and so cause it to crash upon both rescuers and those to be rescued.

This work is done by Rescue Parties, who will also undertake the temporary shoring up or the demolition of partly collapsed buildings where these are a source of immediate danger and the work is within their scope. Rescue Parties are divided into two types, 'Heavy' and 'Light', according to the type of equipment provided. A Heavy party consists of 8 men and a Light party, the duties of which include first aid, of 10 men. Each party is provided also with transport and a driver.

In each type of party the foreman and three others must be skilled men. As it is probable that many of the trapped will be injured, at least four of the six unskilled members of the Light Rescue Parties are also trained and equipped to render first aid in cases when a First Aid Party is not immediately available or requires assistance.

For certain parts of rescue party work, for example the removal by manhandling of piled-up debris, Rescue Parties may be assisted by able-bodied members of the public who offer their assistance at the scene of damage.

DEMOLITION AND REPAIR

After an air raid extensive demolition work may have to be done, streets cleared of wreckage, craters filled in, and fractured gas, water, and electricity mains and sewers may need repair.

Such work may have to be carried out urgently in order to remove danger, or for the purpose of restoring essential services. Work of this kind will be undertaken by parties which are not organized as an Air Raid Precautions Service, but are obtained as required from local authorities' staffs or the staffs of the public utilities concerned, or from contractors, according to the particular work to be undertaken.

In clearing wreckage, demolition and repair parties may, like Rescue Parties, utilize the services of members of the public who offer to help.

UNEXPLODED BOMBS AND WRECKED AIRCRAFT

It may be that bombs from enemy aircraft or shells from our own anti-aircraft guns may fall without exploding. These will be a potential source of danger and will be removed or destroyed by parties specially trained in this work.

Similarly, a crashed enemy aircraft is also dangerous. If it catches fire, the petrol, ammunition, and any bombs still remaining in their racks may explode. If the aircraft is not on fire, there still remains a possible danger of explosion.

It will be the duty of Wardens and the Police to keep the public away from unexploded bombs, shells, and crashed enemy aircraft, and to arrange, as necessary, that nearby buildings should be vacated until the area has been made safe by the appropriate means.

REPORT AND CONTROL CENTRES

For the operation and control of all ARP services, there must be local headquarters to receive damage reports, and to issue instructions for the despatch of the necessary parties to scenes of damage. For this purpose Report and Control Centres have been established. These are manned by telephonists, messengers, clerks, and representatives of the various ARP services, who are co-ordinated by an Officer-in-Charge.

A Report Centre and Control Centre may be combined, or there may be one or more Report Centres linked to the Control Centre. The Control Centre is the nerve-centre of the local organization and the headquarters from which local operations are directed.

ARP CONTROLLERS AND EMERGENCY COMMITTEES

It is essential for the smooth working of the civil defence machinery that local ARP services should be properly co-ordinated and controlled, and that there should exist the necessary co-ordination between these services and the other services of the civil defence organization not incorporated in the air raid precautions organization. For this purpose, and to serve as a channel for giving immediate effect to instructions by the Government and Regional Commissioners, there is in every scheme-making authority's area an ARP Controller, who may be assisted by a Deputy Controller and in some cases by Sub-Controllers.

Major executive decisions regarding the operation of the ARP services are the responsibility of the Controller. Upon his staff are officers of the local authority who are in general charge of the various ARP services, and through these officers instructions are issued to the individual depots and posts. He is also in close touch, either through their presence at the Control Centre or by telephone, with representatives of other Services, such as the police, fire brigades, and medical services, which will be vitally involved in dealing with the effects of air raids.

Associated with the Controller is an Emergency Committee usually consisting of three members of the local Council. Local Councils have delegated extensive powers to Emergency Committees to act on their behalf in matters of civil defence. Under certain conditions of emergency, the Controller may act without first consulting his Committee; in such cases the Committee would be informed after the action had been taken.

The powers of the Controller with regard to matters of civil defence are thus considerable and his responsibilities great, for he must at all times maintain the smooth and efficient working of the various Services of the local organization, and he will be supremely responsible for their operation when raiding takes place.

THINGS TO DO IN AN AIR RAID

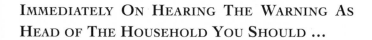

IMMEDIATELY ON HEARING THE WARNING AS
HEAD OF THE HOUSEHOLD YOU SHOULD ...

Personally supervise the following precautions –

1. Send every member of the household immediately to the refuge-room, *making certain that each person has a respirator.*

   Pets should, if possible, have been sent away into the country at the first sign of danger. But if they are still in the house they should be taken into the refuge-room, otherwise they may come into contact with gas, or get splashed by it, and contaminate you. But it should be remembered that animals will help to use up the supply of air in the room. To be on the safe side, count two dogs or cats as one person in choosing the size of your refuge-room.

2. Make some other member of the family, previously appointed for the purpose, responsible for checking that all the articles needed for the refuge-room are properly in place and that the room is properly sealed up against gas, the fire put out, and the chimney blocked up. The blanket over the door should be made damp.

3. Go all round the house, closing all doors and all windows, to reduce the amount of gas which can get into any part of the house.

4. After dark, see that no lights are left burning that may be visible from outside.

5. Extinguish all fires in grates. Fires cause currents of air which may draw in gas from outside. Do not put out these fires with water, as this will fill the house with irritant fumes. Smother them with earth or sand or salt.

6. If you have electric light you may use it, but all gas points that are burning should be turned off. It is better to turn off the gas at the meter, in case the pipes in the house got damaged and began to leak. Do not use gas light or paraffin lamps in the refuge-room, and if you use candles do not burn more at a time than is necessary, to avoid using up oxygen. If the passages to the refuge-room are very dark, you may light them with candles.

7. See that the water buckets or cans which you will have placed about the house are full and ready for use.

When these duties have been seen to, the head of the house or other responsible person should go to the refuge-room, and after making certain that EVERYONE IS THERE SHOULD CLOSE THE DOOR AND SEE THAT THE SEALING ARRANGEMENTS ARE EVERYWHERE INTACT.

If the house is a large one, it would be a good thing for someone to stay outside the refuge-room, on an upper floor or in a trench or dug-out outside, as a watcher in case an incendiary bomb falls on the house or on a neighbouring building. This is not necessary in small houses. The watcher should carry his respirator ready for instant use.

YOU HAVE A HOUSE

YOUR FRIENDS HAVE A HOUSE

YOU MAY LOSE YOURS

BUT THEY'LL PUT YOU UP FOR A TIME

Arrange now with friends or relatives in another part of the town to go to them if *you* are bombed out—and for *them* to come to you if they are bombed out. Your friends can apply for a temporary lodging allowance if they put you up.

FIX THINGS UP NOW

ISSUED BY THE MINISTRY OF HEALTH

WHAT TO DO IN YOUR REFUGE-ROOM

These rules should be closely observed by all persons sheltering in a refuge-room.

1. Sit, or preferably lie down, and keep still, keeping warm with blankets or other coverings.

2. Don't smoke.

3. Don't light fires.

4. Don't go out, unless you must, until you hear the 'Raiders Passed' signal. Be very cautious even then. The danger of gas may not be over although the air raid may have ended. Only one member of the household should go out first to investigate, and he should be wearing his respirator.

5. Pass the time reading, writing, sewing, playing cards or quiet games, listening to the wireless or gramophone. Avoid exertion. Don't let the children romp about as they will only tire themselves out and get exhausted.

6. Do not put on your respirator unless the room is damaged, unless you have to go out, unless you actually smell gas. Remember, too, that a respirator affords no protection against ordinary coal gas.

7. Do not eat food that has come into contact with gas. A food-chest of some kind, or air-tight jars and tins, will guard against this danger.

   Don't forget, on coming out of your refuge-room, that whether the raid is over or not, you may find the rest of the house full of gas. So, except in emergency, keep your family in the refuge-room until you are sure the house is free of gas, or until it has been cleared.

WHAT TO DO IF THE HOUSE IS DAMAGED

At once put on your respirator. If you have to go out of your refuge-room, seek refuge in another room or in another building. If you have to go out of doors keep on your respirator, and wear a mackintosh and goloshes or gum boots if you have them. Avoid all damp splashes on the ground that might be gas. If anyone is injured, a message should be sent to the warden's post, or the nearest first aid party or post.

WHAT TO DO IF FIRE BREAKS OUT

1. Do your best to put the fire out **yourself.**

2. If you cannot do so, summon help at once by calling a fire patrol, air raid warden, or policeman. Have someone on the look-out so that when helpers arrive, you can show them at once where to get to work.

3. See to the safety of all those in the house. If the refuge-room is in danger, get the occupants out. See that they have their respirators on and know what to do.

4. If the gas pipes in the house are damaged, turn the gas supply off at the main, if this has not been done already.

WHAT TO DO WHEN OUT OF DOORS

Always carry a respirator with you throughout the war
If you are out of doors at the time of an air raid, seek shelter at once. If it is impossible to get under cover it is safer to lie on the ground than to stand up, unless you stand in a doorway or narrow archway.

A limited number of public refuges will be available which will provide some protection for those caught in the streets.

Remember other people caught out of doors

If you have any space to spare in your refuge-room, and there is no special reason for not admitting strangers, be ready to take in someone who is caught in the street outside.

WHAT TO DO WHEN YOU COME OUT OF YOUR REFUGE-ROOM

Remember that gas may still be about after the 'Raiders Passed' signal has been sounded.

If you detect gas in your house, keep your refuge-room closed up, but open all the other windows and doors. If you are in doubt, summon an air raid warden.

If you know bombs have fallen close by, go all round the house to see if any damage has been done. Look out of doors to see if your neighbours want any help.

If you have turned off the domestic gas supply at the main, inspect every gas point as soon as you turn it on again to make sure that no tap was left on or has been turned on accidentally.

UNEXPLODED BOMBS

If you know of a bomb which has fallen but has not exploded, tell a policeman or air raid warden at once.

Leave it alone and keep away from it. It may still explode, even some time after it has been dropped. But this does not apply to a small incendiary bomb, which may be carefully picked up, if it is in a building or dangerous place, and carried in a bucket of water to a place of safety.

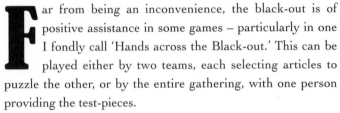

HANDS ACROSS THE BLACK-OUT

Evelyn August

Far from being an inconvenience, the black-out is of positive assistance in some games – particularly in one I fondly call 'Hands across the Black-out.' This can be played either by two teams, each selecting articles to puzzle the other, or by the entire gathering, with one person providing the test-pieces.

The room is plunged in darkness – that should be easy ! – and the person in control begins to hand round a series of objects which the players have to identify entirely from their sense of touch. (Scent and taste are barred.)

If the articles are ingeniously selected, this can be a most up-roarious game. Two suggestions:

A rubber glove filled with sand.

A sponge wrapped in a silk handkerchief.

YOUR REFUGE-ROOM

HOW TO CHOOSE A REFUGE-ROOM

Almost any room will serve as a refuge-room if it is soundly constructed, and if it is easy to reach and to get out of. Its windows should be as few and small as possible, preferably facing a building or blank wall, or a narrow street. If a ground

A cellar or basement is the best position for a refuge-room if it can be made reasonably gas-proof.

In a house with only two floors and without a cellar, choose a room on the ground floor so that you have protection overhead.

floor room facing a wide street or a stretch of level open ground is chosen, the windows should if possible be specially protected. The stronger the walls, floor, and ceiling are, the better. Brick partition walls are better than lath and plaster, a concrete ceiling is better than a wooden one. An internal passage will form a very good refuge-room if it can be closed at both ends.

THE BEST FLOOR FOR A REFUGE-ROOM

A cellar or basement is the best place for a refuge-room if it can be made reasonably gas-proof and if there is no likelihood of its becoming flooded by a neighbouring river that may burst its banks, or by a burst water-main. If you have any doubt about the risk of flooding ask for advice from your local Council Offices.

Alternatively, any room on any floor below the top floor may be used. Top floors and attics should be avoided as they usually do not give sufficient protection overhead from small incendiary bombs. These small bombs would probably penetrate the roof but be stopped by the top floor, though they might burn through to the floor below if not quickly dealt with.

In a two-storeyed terrace house choose a room on the ground floor. The flanking walls will protect you from the blast of a bursting bomb.

In flats or tenement houses, either each household can make its own arrangements or communal refuges can be made. It is, however, important that top-floor dwellers should find accommodation downstairs. They might share a refuge-room, or they might make arrangements to occupy the basement. But the basement premises will have to be prepared as refuges in the same way as ordinary rooms, according to the instructions given in this book.

It is suggested that in any flats, or tenement house, or house occupied by more than one family, representatives be chosen and formed into a Protection Committee to decide upon the most suitable rooms and to prepare them as refuge-rooms if it should ever be necessary for the safety of all.

How Large Should A Refuge-Room Be?

Although an actual raid may be over in a few minutes it might be necessary to stay in your refuge-room for some time, even perhaps for several hours, until the gas in the neighbourhood has been cleared away. You should therefore know how many persons can remain safely in one room without suffering any ill effects. For rooms of normal height (8 to 10 ft) an allowance of 20 square ft of floor area for each person will enable those persons to remain in the room with complete safety for a continuous period of twelve hours *without ventilation.*

A room 10 ft × 10 ft will hold	5 persons.
A room 15 ft × 10 ft will hold	7 persons.
A room 20 ft × 12 ft will hold	12 persons.

If You Cannot Specially Set Aside A Room for A Refuge-Room

You can still make a refuge-room even if you have no surplus room to set aside, in wartime, specially for the purpose. If you have only one room you can make it a place of greater safety – even if you adopt only some of the suggestions contained in this book. Do not think you have no protection. Any room within solid walls is safer than being out in the open, so don't run out into the street to find better shelter if you ever get an air raid warning.

GET THESE THINGS FOR THE REFUGE-ROOM

These are some of the things that will be useful in your refuge-room. Keep them in mind and begin collecting those things you haven't got, one by one. Put them in a box, or in a drawer, in the room you have chosen for your refuge-room.

Things You Probably Possess Already

Candles and matches
Hammer and nails
Scissors

Old newspaper and brown paper
Some clean rags
Needles, cotton, and thread

Things To Collect

A candle lamp, or an electric hand lamp
Suitable material to protect the windows from the blast of an explosion
Gummed paper and adhesive tape
Plywood for blocking the fireplace

A few tins or jars with air-tight lids for storing food

A bottle of disinfectant

A box of First Aid Supplies

If you have a wireless set or receiver it would be useful to have it in the refuge-room so that you could hear the news and pass the time away. Make sure that the plug for it, and the leads for the aerial and earth, if these are required, are made ready.

RENDERING YOUR REFUGE-ROOM GAS-PROOF

The arrows in the picture show the danger points at which gas may enter; these must be sealed as instructed below. Cracks in ceilings and walls should be filled in with putty or pasted over with paper. Cracks between floor boards, round the skirting or where pipes pass through the walls should be filled in with pulp made of sodden newspaper. All ventilators and fireplaces should be stopped up with paper or rags. Windows should be wedged firmly to keep them tight and the frames sealed round with gummed strip or paper. The cracks round doors should be covered with stout paper and the keyhole plugged.

RENDERING YOUR REFUGE ROOM GAS-PROOF

MAKING A DOOR GAS-PROOF

MAKING A DOOR GAS-PROOF

A carpet or blanket should be fixed over the door opening as shown in the illustration. This should be kept wet and at least 12 in. allowed to trail on the floor. Such an arrangement reduces the risk of entry of gas when the door is opened for use. In addition, if there is a large crevice under the door, a wooden strip covered with felt should be nailed to the floor to make a gas-proof joint. The keyhole and all cracks must be stopped up.

PROTECTING YOUR WINDOWS – A SANDBAG DEFENCE

Walls of sandbags or sacks filled with earth, sand, etc., are the best protection for window openings of refuge-rooms on the ground floor. The picture shows how this should be done. Walls should be 2 ft, 6 in. thick at the top and should overlap the window opening by at least 12 in. all round; the base should be wider to prevent the wall collapsing. Such a wall will keep out splinters from high explosive bombs and protect the glass of the window from being shattered by blast. The window must still be sealed against gas.

PROTECTING YOUR WINDOWS—A SANDBAG DEFENCE

FITNESS FOR
LIBERTY!

James A. Milne

At this crucial point in the history of civilization when the barbarian hordes of Nazi-ism are threatening the most ancient outposts of democracy, it behoves a nation to look to its defences. Defences are not alone those of the scientists' and the engineers' creation. Men are units of defence. And as such it is the duty of every man to prepare himself physically and mentally for the struggle that any day may be thrust upon the men of this island. Women, too, are not excluded in this call for preparedness, for the glorious womanhood of the Soviet Union has set a shining example to the women of all other free-thinking freedom-loving lands.

From the grey-haired veterans of the 1914–18 nightmare, now proudly carrying the shoulder numerals of the yet-to-be-tested Home Guard, to the rising youth of the land, Air Training Corps and Boy Scouts too, all are prepared to resist the onslaught of this monstrous army that has already wantonly crushed the greater part of the European continent, prepared in spirit, prepared in certain military and tactical senses. But are they prepared in the physical sense, prepared to stand up to the crushing impact of the *blitzkrieg*, the ceaseless hunting out and rounding up of paratroops that would be their lot in the face of an attempted invasion? And should their time come to take their place along with the standing army in the field would they be able to face up to the long and weary days and nights in the field, days of walking and running, of crawling and of equally exhausting waiting? If they face up to the stark truth they will see that in this sense they are not so fit as they could be.

Physical fitness is the greatest need of today. Those glorious Soviet workers and peasants, whose guerilla tactics in the rear of the German armies dealt such telling blows to the enemy lines of communication and in an equally effective way to the morale of the individual soldier, those men and women were physically fit for the hazardous task which, on the call of their leader, they had joyfully undertaken. The success of their work depended largely on sound physical condition.

For years the greatest criminal band the world has ever known (Adolf Hitler and his followers) have trained the youth of the German nation, trained them mentally in the narrow Nazi creed, but trained them physically to the best of the ability of the best available experts on physical training. And trained with one object, to make them 100 per cent fit units of what Hitler hoped would prove to be the toughest fighting machine in human history. Up to a point the Carrion Crow of Berchtesgaden succeeded. He made them physically tough. But his foul Fascist doctrines could not make them mentally and morally sound.

So now they pay the penalty at the hands of men in whose preparedness there has been a balanced blending of the physical, the mental, and the moral responsibilities.

Where our own men have got to grips with the Nazis, where they have fought the fight out at the point of the bayonet, they too, like their gallant Russian comrades, have proved superior to the Nazis. But these men of ours who have tackled the enemy in close combat have been physically fit, hardened in the tough school of Army training. Not so those who wait but to take their places. Not so those who already have work of defence on hand. It is incumbent on the Home Guard, the NFS in its hours and days of anxious waiting, the ATC, the Boy Scouts, the schools who have been left without masters capable of giving the lads their customary physical training, and the workshop committees, too, to make it a point of duty to see that where a man can be made physically fitter, and therefore mentally and morally sounder, steps should be taken to strengthen the weakness by organizing physical training classes, however brief, however informal.

There was a time when in the lunch-hour the working lads would take off their jackets, tuck their trousers into their socks, and delve into a good half-hour's rough-and-tumble in all-in football. There is less of that nowadays. For one thing the younger men who formed the backbone of the lunch-hour soccer game are now in the Services. The older hands feel that they cannot tackle strenuous exercise on top of a day's hard work. But they are wrong. They are wrong in two senses. They are wrong in that there is no need for the exercise to be strenuous. And they are wrong in thinking that they could not stand up to exercise. On the contrary it would do them a tremendous amount of good, in the end making them much fitter for their daily work. If by becoming fitter they help to increase the production of war materials, they will be doing a service to the nation and to humanity at a time when this should be the first and only consideration of the individual.

The auxiliary Fireman waiting at his post for the coming of the raiders can fill in the frequently boring hours by organizing classes. If there is no room indoors the classes can be taken out in the yard. Air Raid Wardens can get together on the same lines. The Home Guard, the ATC, and the Boy Scouts can set aside at least a couple of evenings a week for voluntary PT And when I say 'voluntary' I mean that the individual is not obliged to attend, but so far as he himself is concerned, he should, as a national duty, make his own attendance compulsory and seek, too, to rope in the slackers – the 'sick, lame and lazy' as we say in the Army.

Let every armoury, every hall, every firestation, every warden's post, every workshop in the land boldly flourish the slogan – FITNESS IN DEFENCE! FITNESS FOR LIBERTY! FITNESS FOR THE FUTURE OF OUR RACE!

'THEIR FINEST HOUR'

Winston Churchill

I do not at all underrate the severity of the ordeal which lies before us, but I believe our countrymen will show themselves capable of standing up to it, like the brave men of Barcelona, and will be able to stand up to it, and carry on in spite of it, at least as well as any other people in the world. Much will depend upon this, and every man and every woman will have the chance to show the finest qualities of their race and render the highest service to their cause. […]

What General Weygand called the 'Battle of France' is over. I expect that the battle of Britain is about to begin. Upon this battle depends the survival of Christian civilization. Upon it depends our own British life and the long continuity of our institutions and our Empire. The whole fury and might of the enemy must very soon be turned on us. Hitler knows that he will have to break us in this island or lose the war. If we can stand up to him all Europe may be free, and the life of the world may move forward into broad, sunlit uplands; but if we fail then the whole world, including the United States, and all that we have known and cared for, will sink into the abyss of a new dark age made more sinister, and perhaps more prolonged, by the lights of

Winston Churchill viewing activity in the Channel from an observation post at Dover Castle during his tour of defences, 28 August 1940.

a perverted science. Let us therefore brace ourselves to our duty and so bear ourselves that if the British Commonwealth and Empire lasts for a thousand years men will still say, 'This was their finest hour'.

18 June 1940

AIR RAID PRECAUTIONS FOR ANIMALS

In cities and towns the larger animals are usually found in congested areas and centres highly vulnerable to enemy aircraft. It may not be generally realized that there are thousands of horses, dogs, and cats in all the big industrial centres, and that in most of them there are also large numbers of cattle (including milch cows), sheep, and pigs.

It has frequently been suggested that general evacuation is desirable, but this is not possible in the case of transport animals (horses) or food animals awaiting slaughter.

In the case of milch cows it is desirable to evacuate them if possible since the difficulties of inward transport of the necessary fodder might be greater than the transport of the milk from outside areas.

Hacks, riding ponies, etc., should be evacuated to rural areas in advance of an emergency.

Dogs and cats and other pets must be considered to be the personal responsibility of their owners. All arrangements should be made in advance owing to the difficulties of transport which are likely to arise at a time of crisis and to the fact that these animals will be prohibited from entering the shelters provided for public use. Owners should make up their minds whether they can

Two men from the People's Dispensary for Sick Animals (PDSA) provide aid for a little boy's dog after London had been hit by the Luftwaffe in April 1941.

take away their dog or cat themselves. If this is impossible they should decide whether the animal is best destroyed or evacuated to the care of friends in the country or to one of the numerous dog and cat homes situated convenient to large cities. [...]

As transportation may entail the congregation of numbers of dogs under unusual and crowded conditions, the provision of well-fitting muzzles is advised in order to prevent injuries that would otherwise arise in these circumstances.

School pets, such as rabbits, guinea-pigs, etc., housed on school premises for the primary training of children in the care of and kindliness to animals will have to be destroyed unless they have been evacuated in advance or satisfactory arrangements have been made to leave them in charge of the caretakers.

PROTECTION OF STABLES

In order to protect animals in their own accommodation, owners should consider the advisability of strengthening as far as possible, stables, cowsheds, kennels, etc., against the dangers arising from high explosives. Nothing except very deep underground stables would give protection against direct hits, and the construction of such accommodation is not likely to be practicable for obvious reasons.

Protection against splinters and blast can be obtained by the proper use of sandbags. [...]

HORSES IN THE STREET

If horses are out at work during a raid the following recommendations are made in order to avoid panic and reduce danger to the public.

Subject to emergency traffic regulations, the horse and vehicle should be removed without delay to a side street or an open space, if this is near, where the horse should be unyoked and tied to a suitable standing. The driver should never attempt to gallop the horse to a place of safety.

Every horse working in the streets during an emergency should be provided with a webbing halter, worn underneath the harness bridle, as an additional control. A halter should be provided with a long lead which will enable the driver to maintain control of his animal while he is engaged in unyoking it. It may also be desirable, in order to assist control, to give a nose-bag feed or in some cases to cover the horse's head so as to obscure vision. This can be done by a hood or a blind fixed to the browband of the bridle. A good driver by remaining beside his horse can often considerably allay the fears of the animal.

In an emergency a driver should undo the halter lead and unyoke. The horse should be tied by the halter lead to a stout tree or to the vehicle and never by the reins. In no case should horses be secured to lamp posts, traffic beacons, or area railings.

If found necessary to tie the animal to a vehicle, it should be secured to the rear, and the vehicle itself anchored with skid brakes, chains, or by other means. In the case of light vehicles, chaining the wheels would be the best method of anchoring the vehicle. The animal in this case should be fastened below the hub of the wheel; by securing low there is less chance of the vehicle being pulled over.

PROTECTION AGAINST GAS

A very real measure of protection is afforded by gas-proofing the stable or byre and no difficulty need be anticipated in the case of well-constructed buildings. Blankets can be used for the inside of the doorways and windows. These can be made to close tightly by means of a felt strip. Small cracks and holes in doors can be filled in with putty, mud, etc. or strong paper may be glued over them. For metal frame windows, gummed paper strip is recommended. Special arrangements must be made for the various types of ventilators, and drainage exits must be stopped – wet hay, wet paperpulp (newspaper), cotton waste or rags are useful for this purpose. Stables and byres can be utilized to the full extent of their floor space and, when gas-proofed, animals will suffer no ill effects if confined in them for a time long enough to ensure the dispersal of non-persistent gases.

In the case of household animals advantage could be taken of the refuge-room. It is recommended that dogs should be muzzled before being taken inside, as any dog may become frenzied during a raid. Where a refuge-room is not available, or, as an additional precaution, the provision of gas-proof boxes may be considered. Unventilated boxes will cause distress to the animal and should not be used. [...]

Birds, domestic pets, and small animals generally should be kept housed during the progress of air raids and subsequently until the ground in the vicinity has been declared safe. Birds are particularly susceptible to gas and therefore their houses or cages should be made gas-proof where possible. It would be useful to cover cages with blankets or sacking, preferably soaked in water.

'GOERING ...
GOERING ... GONE'

A.P. Herbert

And so you think that you can get us down
By vaguely dropping dirt about the town?
Joe Goebbels must have sold you one more pup;
Your sole success has been to get us up.
We'll win the day, whoever steals the night.
You'll get us riled: you'll never get us right.

1 September 1940

Two volunteers for the corps of cyclist ARP messengers.

MANNING THE HOME GUARD

Home Guard Manual

The Home Guard has been organized by the National Service Department, and is, until war conditions obtain, controlled by this Department. The Dominion Headquarters consists of Dominion Commander and a small staff. The Dominion is divided into four **Districts**, each with its Commander and H.Q., and each district into **Areas**, again with their Commanders and H.Q. The areas are subdivided into battalions. Towns will have compact battalions, of four companies and a H.Q. company. Country battalions will consist of scattered units, either sections, platoons or companies, each with a Unit Commander, with an appointment suitable to the size of his unit.

COUNTRY BATTALIONS

As the nature of the operations that the Home Guard is likely to be called on to carry out will involve the manning of isolated section or platoon posts, each unit of the country battalions should train one or two members at least for each of the various jobs of a H.Q. company. For organization purposes battalion H.Q. will establish a skeleton H.Q. company, and the officers of this company will be responsible for the organizing and training

The Home Guard Company for an Arms Factory, 1941.

of their specialist personnel throughout the battalion. Similarly in these battalions, H.Q. should make provision for a staff of instructors, to ensure uniformity of training within the battalion.

ORGANIZATION OF BATTALION, COMPANY AND PLATOON

(I) BATTALION:

H.Q.: Commander.
       Second in Command.
       Adjutant.
       Intelligence Officer.
       Intelligence Section.
       Instructional Staff.
       Regimental Sgt.-Major.
       Regimental Quartermaster-Sgt.
       Six Runners or Cyclists.
       Office Staff.
H.Q. Company.
Four Infantry Companies.

(II) H.Q. COMPANY:

H.Q.: Commander.
       Coy. Sgt.-Major.
       Quartermaster-Sgt.
       Orderly Room Sgt.
       Three Runners.
And five Platoons –
       No. 1, Signals.
       No. 2, Medical.
       No. 3, Transport.
       No. 4, Engineers, and Tank Hunting.
       No. 5, Supplies.

(III) INFANTRY COMPANY:

H.Q. as for H.Q. Coy., with the addition of a Second in Command.

And four Platoons.

(IV) PLATOON:

H.Q.: Commander.
　　　Sergeant.
　　　Two Runners.

And three Sections.

(V) SECTION:

Commander (Corporal).

And seven men, one of whom may be a L/Corporal.

(VI) H.Q. COY. PLATOONS:

(a) **No. 1 Signals:** These signallers will be the specialists. They will equip themselves with flags and lamps, and any other means of communication available (land lines, shutters, etc.). During the 'alert' phase they will, under the direction of the battalion Signals Officer, establish day and night communication with neighbouring units so that signal stations are suitably sited, and their positions known before the second phase begins. They will also reconnoitre the battalion's defence area and site suitable stations, so that communication in the field can be established immediately the third phase begins. The size of the platoon should be sufficient to allow the Coy. Commander to allot two signallers per platoon, while maintaining battalion and company H.Q. stations.

(b) **No. 2 Medical:** The commander will organize one Regimental Aid Post for the battalion, and make provision for four stretcher-bearers per company. All the men should be trained in camp and bivouac sanitation, and take over these duties when conditions require them.

(c) **No. 3 Transport:** Transport must be earmarked for the battalion, including the various branches of the H.Q. company. Road controls must be trained.

(d) **No. 4 Engineers:** Demolition of roads and bridges (on orders from Army), establishment of road-blocks and tank-traps, the construction of temporary bridges, and tank-hunting are the main jobs of this platoon.

(e) **No. 5 Supplies:** This platoon will be required to organize so that on the mobilization of the Home Guard the forwarding of supplies, etc., can operate immediately. They should know what stocks are held locally and where to go for them. They must have a knowledge of the daily supplies necessary for a platoon, and how they are to be sent forward.

EQUIPMENT

It is the responsibility of each unit to equip itself as far as possible. A great deal can be made available locally, and this should be collected in a store at the unit H.Q.

(i) Every man, on mobilization, should bring with him: – A haversack, two blankets, a waterproof coat or sheet, a great-coat, knife, fork, spoon, plate, mug, change of underclothes and socks, a serviceable pair of boots, soap, towel, rations for at least 24 hours, and a bottle of water.

(ii) Gear that can be collected and stored will include: –
Tools of all kinds, buckets, kerosene tins, rope, barbed and
plain wire, pickets and standards, nails and staples, tins
with lids (cocoa, treacle, etc.), thin glass quart bottles and
corks, casks, drums, rags, galvanized iron, etc.

(iii) Supplies can also be earmarked or accumulated and
stored. A typical list will include: – Iron rations, biscuits,
oatmeal, flour, tar, kerosene, petrol, black powder,
gelignite, fuse, matches, detonators, pencils and pads, tea,
coffee, condensed milk, etc.

'THE BIGGEST AND BEST AIR RAID EVER'

Doris Melling

Well, well, well. We had the Biggest and Best air raid ever last night. It was amazing. I have never heard such a row going on in my life.

10.20. Warning. Immediately could hear planes and firing, guns and bombs. Simply terrific. Felt very calm and not the least frightened. Every time I heard a 'crump' I wondered where it had landed. As each plane came over and dropped its bombs, another one appeared. There must have been a good many. Some of the very heavy guns went into action. The wash-house shook like the devil. I thought the Gladstone Dock was getting a pasting. Heard a screaming bomb, but didn't hear it explode. This went on till 2.30 without a break. Just as we thought everything was all clear, they would start up again. Smoked innumerable cigarettes, and felt hungry. Pa kept wanting to have a look out and see if there were any fires. I wouldn't let him. Kept getting annoyed by a few flies which persisted in whizzing round our heads all the time in the shelter. Tried to make out the different noises – which were bombs and which were guns, and where our planes were – if any. I don't think any went up at all. Got to feel cold. Kept wondering when and where it would

Liverpool office girls sort out files and papers on their return to work after the bombing in the blitz.

all end. Every time I heard a fresh plane I wondered where it would drop its load.

About 2.30 a lull set in. One of our planes went over. We returned to the house, and had something to eat, feeling, to say the least, very shaken up, but smiling. We decided we would risk going to bed. I felt very tired. About 3 o'clock the All Clear went. I think they must have waited till they were really satisfied that everything was OK. Could hear people getting home from the pictures. It really is no joke. I shan't go out to the second-house pictures any more. Fell sound asleep.

On the way down to the office this morning everyone was looking out for damage. I never expected anywhere to be standing up, but couldn't see anything much knocked down.

There was nothing to do but stare out of the window, because there were no morning newspapers. Felt rather excited, personally. I think that was a proper raid. I detest sitting in a shelter with nothing happening.

30 August 1940, Liverpool

From 'LONDON PRIDE'

Noël Coward

London Pride has been handed down to us.
London Pride is a flower that's free.
London Pride means our own dear town to us,
And our pride it for ever will be.
Hey, lady,
When the day is dawning
See the policeman yawning
On his lonely beat.
Gay lady,
Mayfair in the morning,
Hear your footsteps echo in the empty street.
Early rain
And the pavement's glistening.
All Park Lane
In a shimmering gown.
Nothing ever could break or harm
The charm of London Town.

INTERLUDE
In our city darkened now, street and square and crescent,
We can feel our living past in our shadowed present,

A balloon barrage for the air defence of London. Each was attached by a steel cable to a winch on the ground by which it could be let up or hauled down to the required height, manned by volunteers with a small nucleus of fully trained regular personnel.

Ghosts beside our starlit Thames
Who lived and loved and died
Keep throughout the ages London Pride.

London Pride has been handed down to us.
London Pride is a flower that's free.
London Pride means our own dear town to us,
And our pride it for ever will be.
Grey city
Stubbornly implanted,
Taken so for granted
For a thousand years.
Stay, city,
Smokily enchanted,
Cradle of our memories and hopes and fears.
Every Blitz
Your resistance
Toughening,
From the Ritz
To the Anchor and Crown,
Nothing ever could override
The pride of London Town.

TAKING SHELTER

GENERAL PRINCIPLES

The first consideration in the provision of a shelter is that it shall give lateral and overhead protection of the approved standard, but there are certain other factors which must also be considered. The most important of these are as follows: –

(I) ENTRANCE AND EXIT

Two entrances, or a main entrance and an emergency exit, should be provided; they should be as far apart as possible, so that both are not likely to be blocked at the same time.

(II) INDEPENDENT LIGHTING

As the normal source of electricity may be damaged, it is important to provide alternative means of lighting. In small shelters torches, or even candles and nightlights, may be used for alternative lighting.

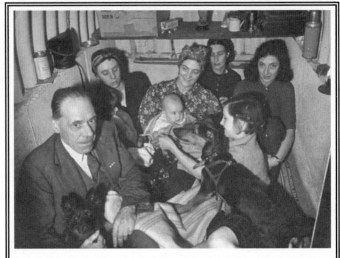

The Mackenzie family sitting during a raid in their Anderson Shelter, 1940.

(III) WATER SUPPLY

A suitable supply of drinking water should be provided.

(IV) FLOODING

Steps should be taken where necessary to prevent ingress of water from damaged water mains in the neighbourhood.

This may be done, for example, by provision of tide boards or by the heightening of parapets round the area. Underground shelter accommodation should not be discarded solely on account of the fear of flooding, if means are provided for the safe escape of its occupants.

(V) SANITARY ARRANGEMENTS

For this purpose, chemical closets may be used if water closets are not available. Some provision, however, is essential.

(VI) TOOLS

A number of tools such as picks, shovels, and crowbars should be kept in a shelter to be used in forcing a way out if the occupants are trapped.

(VII) CONDUCT IN SHELTERS

Vigorous activity in a shelter should be discouraged since it increases the consumption of oxygen and raises the humidity and temperature. Persons in a shelter should, however, be given something to do in order to occupy their minds.

SHELTERS IN BUILDINGS

A reinforced or steel-framed building with concrete roof and floors, and constructed mainly of fire-resisting material, is the safest in which to establish a shelter, because it is less likely to collapse or to catch fire. It is an advantage if a room having a small number of windows can be selected.

Shelters should be situated where the maximum amount of lateral and overhead protection is already available. For this reason, a shelter below ground level provides the best protection against splinters and blast. If suitable accommodation below ground is not available, the ground floor generally provides the best shelter as there is more overhead protection and alternative exits are easier to arrange than in upper storeys. Inner rooms, or rooms the windows of which are masked by neighbouring buildings, internal passages, corridors, and stairwells may also afford satisfactory accommodation. Failing this, an inner room upstairs should be selected, but in such cases there should be at least two floors and the roof of the building above the selected room.

The roof of a shelter should be strengthened to resist the fall of debris in case the superstructure should be demolished. Such strengthening cannot conveniently be improvised on upper floors.

SHELTERS INDEPENDENT OF BUILDINGS

There are many types of outside shelters such as covered trenches, galleries below ground, and shelters lined with steel or concrete, partly above ground level and covered with the necessary thicknesses of earth. Wherever possible these should be sited at a distance from the nearest building of at least half the height of that building. If this is not possible, the roof of the shelter must be strong enough to resist the fall of debris.

(I) TRENCHES

These may be constructed wholly or partly below ground. They afford excellent lateral protection, but they must be given overhead cover against the penetration of light incendiary bombs and of falling splinters from anti-aircraft shells. This requires a head cover of 5 in. of concrete or 18 to 24 in. of earth. More earth should not be used, because, in the event of collapse, the occupants of the shelter might be so deeply buried as to be unable to extricate themselves.

Trenches should provide not less than 6 ft of head room and should be fitted with seats. They must be lined with strong materials to prevent the walls from collapsing, and should be provided with a form of floor covering, such as duckboards or shingle.

Care should be taken to prevent surface water entering the trench. Arrangements must also be made to drain away any water which may seep into the interior of the trench.

(II) GOVERNMENT STEEL SHELTERS ('ANDERSON SHELTERS')

Corrugated steel shelters made in sections to accommodate four or more persons are made to Government specification. These

sections fit together in the form of an arch designed to carry the
necessary covering of earth and also to give protection against
falling debris. Where it is possible to do so, they should be sunk
about 3 ft into the ground and covered with earth to a minimum
depth of 15 in. over the arch. These shelters do not provide the
required standard of protection unless covered by at least this
thickness of earth. The shelter should be sited from 6 to 15 ft
away from a building in such a position that the building protects
the entrance from splinters. Arrangements should be made to
safeguard the shelter against the risk of flooding in wet weather.

(III) SURFACE SHELTERS

These are built entirely above the ground; they may be
constructed of 15 in. of concrete, 12 in. of reinforced concrete, or
13 ½ in. of brickwork. Overhead cover must be provided against

the fall of light incendiary bombs and splinters from anti-aircraft shells, and for this purpose reinforced concrete 5 in. thick may be used. If they are sited nearer a building than half the height of that building, the roof must be strong enough to withstand the weight of falling debris.

LONDON'S DEFIANT SPIRIT

J.B. Priestley

But on these recent nights, when I have gone up to high roofs and have seen the fires like open wounds on the vast body of the city, I've realized, like many another settler here, how deeply I've come to love London, with its misty, twilit charm, its hidden cosiness and companionship, its smoky magic. The other night, when a few fires were burning so fiercely, that half the sky was aglow, and the tall terraces around Portland Place were like pink palaces in the Arabian Nights, I saw the Dome and Cross of St Paul's, silhouetted in sharpest black against the red flames and orange fumes, and it looked like an enduring symbol of reason and Christian ethics seen against the crimson glare of unreason and savagery. 'Though giant rains put out the sun, here stand I for a sign.'

In a supreme battle for the world's freedom, there can be no doubt that you and I are now in the midst of such a battle, there are only two capital cities in the world that are worthy of figuring in its portrait – one of them is Paris, city of quick barricades and revolutions, now temporarily out of the fight, not because its brave people lost heart but rather because they lost interest and so allowed banal men, intriguers greedy for wealth and power and all the enemies of a people on the march, to deceive and betray them.

The City of London, with St Paul's Cathedral swathed in smoke, after a bombing raid.

The other city is great London, which during the last thousand years – and what are the wobblings and timidities of the last ten years compared with the nine hundred and ninety that went before – has many a time given itself a shake and risen to strike a blow for freedom, and not only its own freedom but that of men everywhere. In this capacity, as any European history book will show you, it is in sharp contrast to Berlin which has never yet been regarded as a beacon light by the free spirit of mankind. But London has often been seen as such a beacon light. Even the chief revolutionaries of our time lived here in their day and were nourished on books paid for by London citizens. And now, in the darkest hour, it blazes again; yes, because the incendiary bombs have been rained upon it but also because its proud defiance and unconquerable spirit have brought to men and women all over the world renewed hope and courage.

This, then, is a wonderful moment for us who are here in London, now in the roaring centre of the battlefield, the strangest army the world has ever seen, an army in drab civilian clothes, doing quite ordinary things, an army of all shapes and sizes and ages of folk, but nevertheless a real army, upon whose continuing high and defiant spirit the world's future depends.

Much has been made, both here and overseas, of the fine courage and resolution of the London citizen, and especially of all the people in the various air raid services, and our most inspiring voice, that of the Prime Minister, has told us of our high destiny. But I venture to think that not enough has been made of two facts. First, that we are not civilians who have happened to stray into a kind of hell on earth, but that we are soldiers fighting a battle. And this isn't a mere figure of speech and shouldn't be regarded as such, because I am certain it would be wiser to treat persons doing essential work in certain areas on a military basis, removing all people not doing essential work from such areas and providing the rest, the front-line troops of our battle of London, with all necessary shelter, food and transport.

Some of us said long before this *blitzkrieg* began that the pretence that life was more or less normal for everybody was a very dangerous one. It's better to say outright, now we're all going to have a jolly good shake up, but only in order to carry on all the better. Most people don't mind that – they rather like it, but, of course, nobody likes being bombed at all odd hours; to go home as I did the other morning at dawn and notice that a large bus has been flattened like a tin toy against the second storey of a building, is to feel, to say the least of it, that things are becoming most rum and peculiar. Which brings me to the second fact that's been understressed. It is that we have not suddenly entered upon a new and quite lunatic way of living with the prospect of months and months and months of sirens and shelters and bombs before us (which is what some authorities appear to imagine), but that we have been flung into a battle – a real terrific honest-to-God battle – perhaps the most important this war will see, and that, therefore, we must summon up all the courage and resolution and cheerfulness we possess and stick it out until the battle is over. As a kind of civilian life this is hellish, but as battles go, it is not at all bad – with some shelter, meals arriving fairly regularly and a quick rescue of the wounded. But I am not giving this advice to the cockneys – they don't need any from me, only an apology for ever imagining their old spirit had left them, and a stare of admiration. They can say to Herr Hitler and Marshal Goering (who really will have to read *Pickwick*) what Sam Weller said: 'Sorry to keep you waiting, Sir, but I'll attend to you directly.'

HALT, ADVANCE, DEPLOY

Home Guard Manual

(A) SIGNALS WITH THE HAND

NOTES –

(a) All hand signals are preceded by a short blast of the whistle.

(b) In field drill no action is carried out following a signal until the hand is cut to the side.

(i) **DEPLOY:** Arm extended over the head and waved slowly from side to side, the hand coming as low as the hips on each side.

To signal 'Deploy to a flank' the arm is extended in the direction of that flank before being lowered.

(ii) **ADVANCE:** Arm swung from rear to front below the shoulder.

(iii) **HALT:** Arm raised to full extent above the head, hand open.

(iv) **RETIRE:** Arm circled above head.

(v) **CHANGE DIRECTION RIGHT (LEFT):** Arm extended in line with shoulder, then a circular movement made; on completion body and arm point in the required direction.

A Home Guard detachment patrolling along cliff paths near Dover or Folkestone, March 1941.

(vi) **RIGHT (LEFT) TURN (INCLINE):** Body turned in required direction, and arm extended shoulder high, pointing in the required direction.

(vii) **CLOSE:** Hand placed on top of the head, elbow square to right or left, according to which hand is used.

This signal means close on the centre. To close on a flank, the leader will point to the required flank before dropping his hand.

If, on the march, it is required to halt as well as close, the halt signal will be given before the hand is dropped.

(viii) **QUICK TIME:** Hand raised in line with shoulder, elbow bent and close to the side.

(ix) **DOUBLE:** Clenched hand moved up and down between shoulder and thigh.

(x) **LIE DOWN:** Two or three slight movements with the open hand, palm downwards, toward the ground.

(xi) **AS YOU WERE, WASH-OUT, BREAK OFF:** Arm extended downwards with the hand open, and waved across the body parallel with the ground.

(xii) **LAST ORDER COMPLETED:** The salute, followed by the hand raised vertically above the head, hand open and fingers together.

(xiii) **ENEMY AIRCRAFT IN SIGHT:** Both arms held above the head and the hands waved.

(B) SIGNALS WITH THE RIFLE

(i) **ENEMY IN SIGHT IN SMALL NUMBERS:** Rifle held above the head at the full extent of the arm, parallel with the ground, muzzle pointing to the front.

(ii) **ENEMY IN SIGHT IN LARGE NUMBERS:** The rifle held as in previous signal, but raised and lowered frequently.

(iii) **NO ENEMY IN SIGHT:** The rifle held up to the full extent of the arm, muzzle pointing up.

A classic poster from the time, with a sentiment that is still popular.

A woman saving board games from bomb wreckage, London, 1939–1945.

ANTI-AIRCRAFT SEARCHLIGHT The duty of an anti-aircraft searchlight units is to find and illuminate enemy aircraft so that they can be attacked by our own fighter machines or fired at by anti-aircraft guns. The searchlight has a glass paraboloid reflector 36in. in diameter and an electric arc lamp which gives a light of many millions of candle power. In fine weather the searchlight has a range of over 5 miles. The complete searchlight detachment consists of ten men who work the searchlight, a sound locator and a generating plant which provides the necessary power for the arc lamp.

A GARDEN DUG-OUT The picture shows a dug-out which is gas-proof and will give protection from blast and splinters from high explosive bombs. The excavation is in the form of a trench 7 ft deep and 6 ft wide at the top and 4 ft wide at the bottom. The earth sides are supported by corrugated iron sheets held in place by uprights as shown in the picture. The roof consists of corrugated iron sheets resting on wooden joists laid across the excavation. Inside the entrance is an air lock formed by two gas curtains. Outside the dug-out, steps lead down from one side to the entrance.

January 1941. Firemen attempt to keep a blaze under control.

September 1939. Londoners prepare for aerial attack, removing valuables and important documents, and sandbagging buildings against the bomb attacks they expect.

What to do about GAS

In a gas attack, first put on your own mask, then you will be better able to help baby.

HINTS TO MOTHERS

★ Learn to put on baby's gas helmet quickly, while wearing your own mask. Your Health Visitor will show you how. If you don't know her address ask at Town Hall or at the Child Welfare Centre.

★ With more than one baby you need help. Arrange with a neighbour, or find out if your local W.V.S. has a Housewives' Service.

★ Toddlers soon learn to put on their own masks. Let them make a game of it and they will wear their gas masks happily.

MAKE SURE YOUR FAMILY HAVE THEIR GAS MASKS WITH THEM NIGHT & DAY

Invaluable instructions for protecting children, even if the chaos of bombing sometimes made them unrealistic.

The inspirational Winston Churchill at his most belligerent.

Residents inspect bomb damage in 1943. Battersea power station can be seen in the background.

A flag still hangs defiantly beside a bombed-out London shop. The graffiti on the right sums up the Blitz Spirit.

(C) SIGNALS WITH WHISTLE

(i) **CAUTIONARY BLAST** (a short blast): To call attention to a signal or order about to be given.

(ii) **RALLY BLAST** (succession of short blasts): To denote 'Close on the leader' when a signal cannot be seen. Men double towards the sound of the whistle.

(iii) **ALARM BLAST** (succession of alternating long and short blasts): To turn out troops from camp or bivouac to fall in or to occupy previously arranged positions.

(iv) **ENEMY AIRCRAFT IN SIGHT** (a succession of long blasts): On this signal troops either get ready to engage the aircraft, or open out and take cover, according to previous orders.

(v) **AIRCRAFT ATTACK ENDED** (two long blasts repeated at intervals of five seconds).

'BAD NIGHTS, WORSE NIGHTS, AND BETTER NIGHTS'

Mollie Panter-Downes

For Londoners, there are no longer such things as good nights; there are only bad nights, worse nights, and better nights. Hardly anyone has slept at all in the past week. The sirens go off at approximately the same time every evening, and in the poorer districts, queues of people carrying blankets, thermos flasks, and babies begin to form quite early outside the air raid shelters. The *Blitzkrieg* continues to be directed against such military objectives as the tired shopgirl, the red-eyed clerk, and the thousands of dazed and weary families patiently trundling their few belongings in perambulators away from the wreckage of their homes. After a few of these nights, sleep of a kind comes from complete exhaustion. The amazing part of it is the cheerfulness and fortitude with which ordinary individuals are doing their jobs under nerve-racking conditions. Girls who have taken twice the usual time to get to work look worn when they arrive, but their faces are nicely made up and they bring you a cup of tea or sell you a hat as chirpily as ever. Little shopkeepers whose windows have been blown out paste up 'Business as usual' stickers and exchange cracks with their customers. [...]

The East End suffered most in the night raids this week. Social workers who may have piously wished that slum areas could be razed had their wish horribly fulfilled when rows of mean dwellings were turned into shambles overnight. The Nazi attack bore down heaviest on badly nourished, poorly clothed people – the worst equipped of any to stand the appalling physical strain, if it were not for the stoutness of their cockney hearts. Relief workers sorted them out in schools and other centres to be fed, rested, and provided with billets. Subsequent raids killed many of the homeless as they waited.

The bombers, however, made no discrimination between the lowest and the highest homes in the city. The Queen was photographed against much the same sort of tangle of splintered wreckage that faced hundreds of humbler, anonymous housewives in this week's bitter dawns. The crowd that gathered outside Buckingham Palace the morning after the picture was published had come, it appeared on close inspection, less to gape at boarded windows than to listen to the cheering notes of the band, which tootled away imperturbably at the cherished ceremony of the Changing of the Guard. This was before the deliberate second try for the Palace, which has made people furious, but has also cheered them with the thought that the King and Queen are facing risks that are now common to all. [...]

14 September 1940

After a fortnight of savage nocturnal bombardments, Londoners are settling down with courage and resource to live by a completely new timetable. The big stores and many of the offices now close an hour earlier in order to give workers a chance to get home and have a meal before the uncomfortable evening programme begins, which it does with unfailing regularity.

Getting home is a tricky business for those who live in the suburbs, for bomb damage and rush hours at unexpected times of day have put a strain on the transport services. Lucky commuters have been cadging lifts from passing motorists and lorry-drivers; the not-so-lucky have been doggedly hiking rather than risk being caught out in the night air, which definitely isn't healthy just now, as much because of the terrific anti-aircraft barrages as because of bombs.

Families of modest means who have no cellars in their homes and perhaps don't care to trust to their Anderson Shelters start queuing up outside the public shelters as early as six in the evening, with their bundles of bedding and their baskets of food. Thousands more turn the tube stations into vast dormitories every night – a kind of lie-down strike which at first perplexed the authorities, who could not think what to do with passengers who paid their three-hapence and then proceeded to encamp quietly on the platforms. Since these folk have given no trouble and haven't, as was feared, cluttered up the corridors to the inconvenience of passengers with a genuine urge to get somewhere, the latest semi-official ruling is that the practice can be continued. The Ministries of Transport and Home Security, however, have appealed to the public not to use the tube as a shelter except in cases of urgent necessity. The urgent necessity of many of the sleepers who doss down on the platforms nightly is that they no longer have homes to go to; each morning, more are leaving their underground sanctuary to go back and find a heap of rubble and splinters where their houses used to be. The bravery of these people has to be seen to be believed. They would be heart-rending to look at if they didn't so conspicuously refuse to appear heart-rending. Their reaction has taken the form of anger, and there is a good deal of hopeful talk about smashing reprisals on Berlin. Anger has probably been responsible for a recent rise in munitions production. Hundreds of men and women are working a bit faster as they think of those heaps of rubble.

Bombs of heavy calibre were dropped in some of this week's raids, and time bombs were also extensively used. A new headache for householders is the possibility of being evacuated with only a few minutes' warning, as they must be when a time bomb falls anywhere near. The most heroic among the millions of heroic workers in London these days are the Royal Engineers, who deal in squads with time bombs, going down into the craters and working with mathematical nicety. The squad which saved St Paul's naturally came in for much deserved publicity, but there are plenty of equally courageous groups risking their lives daily with the same coolness, if under less spectacular circumstances. The auxilary fire services, too, have done magnificent work, and an announcement of civilian-service decorations which will be the equivalent of military honors is expected shortly. Firemen, wardens, Home Guards, and nurses alike were killed while on duty during this week's raids. Nurses have been under fire constantly, for several hospitals have been hit more than once. St Thomas's, on the river opposite the Houses of Parliament (which presumably were the target), is a tragic sight, its wards ripped open by bombs.

The bombers have turned their attention to the West End for the last few nights and the big stores have suffered heavily. John Lewis & Co. and others were badly damaged, but one gutted building looks much like another, and Londoners, after a brief glance, go briskly on to work. Taxi-drivers grumble about the broken glass, which is hard on their tyres, and about the difficulty of navigating in neighborhoods which they know like the backs of their hands but which may overnight become

Clearance and repair of bomb damage, King Street, Hammersmith, 1940

unrecognizable. All the same, their grumbles have the usual cockney pithiness and gaiety, and taxis get you home in spite of anything short of a raid right overhead. Gaiety does turn up even in such grim days. It was funny to see raw sirloins of beef being carried from one stately club, which was temporarily cut off from its gas supply, to another equally stately establishment, which had offered the hospitality of its old-fashioned coal ranges; it was funny to see a florist's beautifully arranged hot-house blossoms waving in a stiff breeze that blew through the shattered windows of his shop.

21 September 1940

'WE COULD SEE LITTLE PUFFS OF SMOKE'

Joan Wilshin

… Then we went into St James's Park for the rest of the afternoon, and we were just thinking about going somewhere for tea when the sirens went, so we stopped in the Park, & did we get a good view of it. Honestly, Jerry planes seemed to come over by the thousand, we could see little puffs of smoke in the sky where they were firing at one another, we could hear bombs dropping all round. When they fired the guns in Hyde Park, they nearly shot us in the Serpentine, talk about exciting, I wouldn't have missed it for anything. Then when the All Clear went, we just had time to get a cup [of] tea before going to a show. […] Of course, the sirens had to go again in the middle of it, but they carried on with the show so we stopped to the end, but when we came out you should have seen the sky. That big fire was just about at its worst, it was lit up for miles. All the buses were stopped & the tubes, so we had to walk from Shaftesbury Avenue to Marylebone Station. There wasn't a soul about, we could hear singing coming up from most of the shelters as we passed them, so they seemed to be making the best of a bad job. We eventually got to Marylebone in safety although just as we arrived there was a terrific explosion & we learnt afterwards it was a bomb fallen

Fire-watching duty on the roof of Hulton Press. Behind the two men can be seen the City of London, including the Old Bailey and St Paul's Cathedral.

in Euston Rd so that wasn't far off. They made us go into a shelter until the train came and I eventually got home about 1am, none the worse for it all.

DANCING THROUGH

n 18 November came the 'Black-out Stroll', the first distinctly war dance produced during the war, about which the first publicity said:

> You ladies called 'wallflowers', fated to sit out all the dances, because perhaps your face isn't your fortune, or you aren't too good a dancer, or your figure isn't the cuddly kind … HERE'S YOUR CHANCE TO DANCE THE 'BLACK-OUT STROLL', LONDON'S LATEST STEP IS YOUR GODSEND…

You start dancing with a partner, doing forward walking steps, a break-away (much toned-down jitterbug step), and 1, 2, 3, hop (the Romp), then more walking steps. The lights go out, and when they go on again you are dancing with somebody else.

> How's that help you, wallflowers?
> Dash it, you aren't dumb, are you?

But apparently some of them are, for when an observer watched the dance at a West-End ballroom, of the forty couples on the floor (about the average that evening for a quickstep – most

Railway poster produced during the Second World War to remind passengers about safety when opening carriage doors and alighting from trains.

popular dance), only about a quarter broke away when the lights went out, and some of those had to dance together again, because there were no wallflowers waiting to grab the men.

Composer Tommie Connor told an observer:

My main reason for getting the dance out was to get one which would allow a change of partner, and also bring an atmosphere of jollity on to the dance-floors. There has been a 75 per cent change of face in the ballroom since the war began. Evacuees are going into ballrooms which they have never been in before. This gives them the party-spirit, which was somehow missing in the dance-hall after the war. My dance makes them happier. It gives everyone a reason to meet everyone else.

And why not? For

There's no more cuddling in the moonlight,
There's no more petting in the park.
But why let's worry over moonlight?
For when we're strolling in the dark IT'S LOVELY.
Everybody do the 'Black-out Stroll';
Laugh and drive your cares right up the pole.
Whisper, 'See ya later', to your baby doll,
For now we change our partners in the 'Black-out Stroll.'

Black-out had already been the subject of a new version of the 'Lambeth Walk' by Al Bollington, pilot in the RAF reserve and famous BBC organist. He wrote it a week or two after war commenced, and played it to cinema-goers before they left his theatre, with the following words:

Down the inky avenue,
Inky, pinky, parlez vous.
You'll find your way
Doing the 'Black-out Walk', Oi!

And so on, including 'Keep on smiling, don't be blue; don't let Hitler worry you.'

The staff of C. & A. Modes in Manchester developed another 'Lambeth Walk' version of their own:

When you hear the whistle blow
Down to the basement you must go;
You'll find them all
Doing the Air Raid Walk.

(Evening Chronicle, 14 September)

LONDON'S HOUR

Vera Brittain

That night three hospitals and a number of churches are struck by bombs; 30 ft of a steeple in West London becomes a heap of rubble and debris. A famous hotel is hit, and a Colonel and his wife who were sleeping in the damaged quarter are killed. Within a quarter-mile radius in Central London, every pane of glass in shops and houses is shattered. Fire breaks out at the bottom of one main thoroughfare, saving the Nazi airmen the trouble of dropping flares over our district. Fifty yards from my flat, two houses in an adjacent crescent get direct hits and collapse with a roar; as I hear the bombs scream past our windows, the solid building above me cracks and shudders until I feel that the mass of steel and concrete is descending on my head. Sleepless after the tumult of the night, I go out at 7.30am into a calm sunny morning, and observe the smoke from an incendiary bomb which is still smouldering on the roof of the flats opposite our own.

That afternoon a friend and I attend, as visitors and observers, an Emergency Relief Committee convened by the Society of Friends at an East End Settlement close to the Bow Road, where a vigorous group of young men from a Quaker training centre in

LOOK
before you sleep
ALL WINDOWS AND INNER DOORS OPEN?
WATER IN BUCKETS?
WATER
WATER
SAND IN BUCKETS?
SAND
SAND
GAS MASK, CLOTHES AND TORCH HANDY?
GOOD NIGHT!

Birmingham has arrived to help in tackling the social problems created by the bombing of the crowded boroughs. As the usual route is now out of action, we make our way to the Bow Road by a complicated series of much-impeded conveyances.

'Thank God,' I think, as we drive between its damaged houses, 'that "Uncle George" has passed beyond reach of the grief which the suffering of his old constituency would have caused him!'

Just as we arrive, the siren goes for the hundredth time, and our committee meeting is held in a white-washed dug-out beneath the Settlement, with a concrete ceiling and cushions on the floor.

Only a few days earlier, an aerial torpedo has fallen just outside the Settlement, turning the surrounding region into a devastated area which I can now compare without reservation to the shattered towns that I saw in France at the end of the last war. It is hardly surprising that we share our business meeting with a number of mothers and small children who seek refuge in the friendly shelter. For some reason I am reminded of Swinburne's poem, 'Watchman, what of the night?' If anything can give assurance that dawn will someday come, it is the tranquil determination of the Quaker leader, John Hoyland, and his group of young men, to do what they can towards clearing up the chaos brought to London's poorest districts by the generations of irresponsible politicians who never really believed that they who sow the wind must reap the whirlwind.

The Committee is reluctantly obliged to conclude that the problem of the East End – its wrecked houses, its homeless families, its inadequate surface shelters which should have been deep and the increasingly grim conditions inside them – is one of such magnitude that only the Government itself, or bodies such as

Shelterers read the paper and prepare for sleep in a dimly-lit tunnel of the London Underground network, probably at Aldwych in November 1940.

the London County Council and the local authorities, possess sufficient resources to tackle it on a scale which can be efffective. Already the raided populations, against the will of the Government, have taken possession of the Underground Railways, which are excavated so far below the earth that no bomb can reach them. Night after night, men, women and children equipped with rugs, mattesses and cushions, queue up patiently at the gateways to these unofficial shelters which represent the only security that they in their poverty and helplessness, have power to commandeer. It is beyond the scope of voluntary organizations to do more than ameliorate their needs, though they can usefully put pressure on lethargic authorities to take defence measures which should have been started months ago.

Feeling too weary to struggle again with the complications of shattered Tube and 'bus routes, my friend and I return by taxi to the comparative presentableness of Marylebone. Our journey back through the East End and the City resembles a nightmare fantasy by H.G. Wells. In the Mile End Road, every other house seems to have been demolished; again and again we encounter forlorn little processions of office workers, suitcases in hand, who have been driven from their homes or business premises by time bombs. The narrow City streets involve a maze of temporary detours; craters in the roads are surrounded by uncleared heaps of bricks and stones; yawning gaps appear where banks and warehouses have stood. In the Euston Road we run into a traffic-block which crawls towards Marylebone. Eventually, in spite of the skeleton of Madame Tussaud's and the blackened façade of Chiltern Court, we feel that we have returned to civilization. Soon we are to learn that the remnants of civilization are themselves only temporary.

HOW TO WEAR YOUR GAS MASK

The Civilian Respirator consists of a face-piece, to which is attached by means of a rubber band a metal box containing filters which will absorb all known war gases. The face-piece is held in position by means of web straps fitting round the head. When the respirator is properly fitted and the straps adjusted, it completely protects the eyes, nose, mouth and lungs. The strap should be pinned at the right tension, so that the respirator can be slipped on in an instant. This respirator will be issued free to the public.

THE CIVILIAN RESPIRATOR

THE CIVILIAN DUTY RESPIRATOR

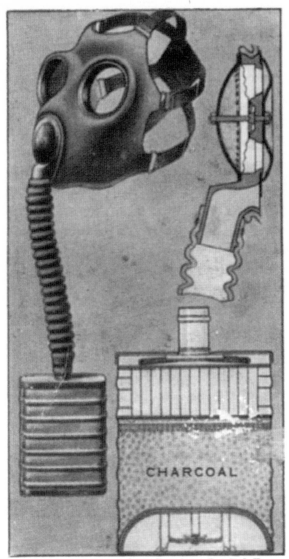

THE SERVICE RESPIRATOR

The Civilian Duty Respirator is of stronger construction than the Civilian Respirator and is intended for those who might have to work in the presence of gas and could not go to a gas-protected refuge-room. The respirator protects the eyes, nose, mouth and lungs against all known war gases. The face-piece is of moulded rubber, and the eye-pieces are of strong glass. There is an outlet valve opposite the nose; the protuberance at the side of the face-piece can be used to fit a microphone for speaking on the telephone.

The Service Respirator is designed for the fighting services. It will also be used by members of those civil Air Raid Precautions services who might have to perform strenuous duties to perform in heavy gas concentrations. This respirator gives the same protection as the Civilian Respirator but for a longer period. It is designed so that the weight of the container portion is carried in the haversack on the chest, and the special face-piece allows heavy and accurate work to be performed without difficulty.

THE BOMBARDMENT CONTINUES

Harold Nicolson

DIARY

26 August 1940

A lovely morning. They raided London yesterday and we raided Berlin. I work at my broadcast talk. At noon I hear aeroplanes and shortly afterwards the wail of the siren. People are really becoming quite used to these interruptions. I find one practises a sort of suspension of the imagination. I do not think that the drone in the sky means death to many people at any moment. It seems so incredible as I sit here at my window [at Sissinghurst] looking out on the fuchsias and the zinnias with yellow butterflies playing round each other, that in a few seconds above the trees I may see other butterflies circling in the air intent on murdering each other. One lives in the present. The past is too sad a recollection and the future too blank a despair.

Dine at the Beefsteak. An air raid warning sounds. I wait till 10.45 and then walk back to K.B.W. It is a strange experience. London is as dark as the stage at Vicenza after all the lights have been put out. Vague gleamings of architecture. It is warm and stars straddle the sky like grains of rice. Then there are bunches in the corners of searchlights, each terminating in a swab of cotton wool which is its own mist area. Suburban guns thump and boom. In the centre there are no guns, only the drone of aeroplanes which may be enemy or not. A few lonely footsteps hurry along the Strand. A little nervous man catches up with me and starts a conversation. I embarrass him by asking him to have a cigarette and pausing lengthily while I light it. His hand trembles. Mine does not. I walk on to the Temple and meet no one.

When I get into my rooms, I turn the lights off and sit at the window. There is still the drone of planes and from time to time a dull thump in the distance. I turn on my lights and write this, but I hear more planes coming and must darken everything and listen. I have no sense of fear whatsoever. Is this fatalism or what? It is very beautiful. I wait and listen. There are more drones and then the search lights switch out and the All Clear goes. I shut my shutters, turn on my lights and finish this. The clocks of London strike midnight. I go to bed.

19 September 1940

I get sleepy and go back to my room. I turn out the lights and listen to the bombardment. It is continuous, and the back of the museum opposite flashes with lights the whole time. There are scudding low clouds, but above them the insistent drone of the German 'planes and the occasional crump of a bomb. Night after night, night after night, the bombardment of London continues. It is like the Conciergerie, since every morning one is pleased to see one's friends appearing again. I am nerveless, and yet I am conscious that when I hear a motor in the empty streets I tauten myself lest it be a bomb screaming towards me. Underneath, the fibres of one's nerve-resistance must be sapped. There is a

City of Westminster.

AIR RAID SHELTERS
AT NIGHT

See the BLUE LIGHT-
- it means
SHELTER at NIGHT

Issued by Westminster City Council, A.R.P. Office, Alhambra House, 31, Charing Cross Rd., W.C.2. 12th January 1940.

lull now. The guns die down towards the horizon like a thunderstorm passing to the south. But they will come back again in fifteen minutes. We are conscious all the time that this is a moment in history. But it is very like falling down a mountain. One is aware of death and fate, but thinks mainly of catching hold of some jutting piece of rock. I have a sense of strain and unhappiness; but none of fear.

One feels so proud.

24 September 1940

I detect in myself a certain area of claustrophobia. I do not mind being blown up. What I dread is being buried under huge piles of masonry and hearing the water drip slowly, smelling the gas creeping towards me and hearing the faint cries of colleagues condemned to a slow and ungainly death.

8 October 1940

Go round to see Julian Huxley [then Secretary of the Zoological Society] at the Zoo. He is in an awkward position since he is responsible for the non-escape of his animals. He assures me that the carnivores are pretty safe although a zebra got out the other day when its cage had been bombed and bolted as far as Marylebone. While we were at supper a fierce raid begins and the house shakes. The raid gets very bad and at 8.30 he offers to drive me back. It is a heavenly moon-lit night and the search-lights are swaying against a soft mackerel sky and a clear calm moon. The shells lit up their match flares in the sky. A great star shell creeps slowly down over the city under a neat parachute. We hear loud explosions all round but he gets out his car and drives me back bravely to the Ministry.

Members of the London Fire Brigade train their hoses on burning buildings in Queen Victoria Street, London, after the last and heaviest major raid mounted on the capital during the Blitz, on the night of 10/11 May 1941, when aircraft of the Luftwaffe dropped over 1,000 tons of bombs on London.

14 February 1941

Dear London! So vast and unexpectant, so ugly and so strong! You have been bruised and battered and all your clothes are tattered and in disarray. Yet we, who never knew that we loved you (who regarded you, in fact, like some old family servant, ministering to our comforts and amenities, and yet slightly incongruous and absurd), have suddenly felt the twinge of some fibre of identity, respect and love. We know what is coming to you. And our eyes slip along your old untidy limbs, knowing that the leg may be gone tomorrow, and that tomorrow the arm may be severed. Yet through all this regret and dread pierces a slim clean note of pride. 'London can take it.' I believe that what will win us this war is the immense central-dynamo of British pride. The Germans have only assertiveness to put against it. That is transitory. Our pride is permanent, obscure and dark. It has the nature of infinity.

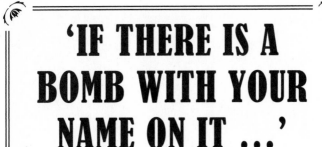
veryone I have met since our three-night bombardment all had the same expression on their lips, namely, 'Wasn't it awful?' A strained looking-ahead expression as much as to say, 'Will it be my turn next?' A certain type of person, in fact I think the larger percentage of people now, shrug their shoulders, mentally and physically and say, 'If there is a bomb with your name on it, it will get you, shelter or no shelter.'

For myself I find the intensified bombing gradually coming closer intensifies one's feelings. As the planes drone nearer, the bombs drop nearer, the ack-ack start up, the shelter quiet, my husband and child asleep, everything seems clear before my eyes. My thoughts turn with gratitude to the goodness of God for preserving me and mine. I realize what the other people are suffering, the people now under the power of the SS men, I push it into the background and it comes out in my dreams. [...]

Always I like everything ready to go straight down to the shelter if there is a warning. If there is a meal imminent I lay it on the tray as I prepare it. If we are expecting a raid we sit down

EQUIPPING YOUR REFUGE ROOM—A

to the table with the meal on the tray but if we are all having a meal I lay the table and have the tray handy where I can just put the things on it. Our eating habits are just the same. I prepare for myself and child and separately for my husband. [...]

After looking inside heaps of shelters I have decided that mine is as much like home as anyone's. I bought a 'Spiral divan' just before the war for taking up and down when we had visitors so that it would leave my child's bedroom freer in between times. Fortunately it fits just into the length of the shelter, it is 2 ft wide which just leaves room for J.'s little bed at the side which consists of my padded deck chair put very low and levelled up with cushions and a footboard. We have 18 in. square to stand in, fortunately we are both slight.

My husband has fixed 4 hooks for us and a bullet-proof steel door which we can lock. He has also made us a candle-holder out of a 6*d* gas mask container and arranged it so that it can slip into a holder on the wall. [...] The condensation is the biggest problem, the walls run damp and wet as soon as the atmosphere becomes humid. My underneath mattress soaked up all that but left the rest of the shelter bone dry. I have decided to have the mattresses changed over every two days and so ensure that we don't get rheumatism by bringing them in and airing them. From what my neighbours say, having the divan on legs I have the benefit of being able to keep a tin of emergency rations underneath, about 12/6∂ worth, my leather case with all important papers in and first aid.

Birmingham

'WE MUST BE UNDAUNTED'

Winston Churchill

A month has passed since Herr Hitler turned his rage and malice on to the civil population of our great cities and particularly of London. He declared in his speech of 4 September that he would raze our cities to the ground, and since then he has been trying to carry out his fell purpose. […] It would seem that, taking day and night together, nearly 400 of these machines [long-range German bombers] have, on the average, visited our shores every 24 hours. […]

Neither by material damage nor by slaughter will the people of the British Empire be turned from their solemn and inexorable purpose. It is the practice and in some cases the duty of many of my colleagues and many Members of the House to visit the scenes of destruction as promptly as possible, and I go myself from time to time. In all my life, I have never been treated with so much kindness as by the people who have suffered most. One would think one had brought some great benefit to them, instead of the blood and tears, the toil and sweat which is all I have ever promised. On every side, there is the cry, 'We can take it' but with it, there is also the cry, 'Give it 'em back'. […]

As I see it, we must so arrange that, when any district is smitten by bombs which are flung about at utter random, strong,

mobile forces will descend on the scene in power and mercy to conquer the flames, as they have done, to rescue sufferers, provide them with food and shelter, to whisk them away to places of rest and refuge, and to place in their hands leaflets which anyone can understand to reassure them that they have not lost all, because all will share their material loss, and in sharing it, sweep it away. […]

Because we feel easier in ourselves and see our way more clearly through our difficulties and dangers than we did some months ago, because foreign countries, friends or foes, recognize the giant, enduring, resilient strength of Britain and the British Empire, do not let us dull for one moment the sense of the awful hazards in which we stand. Do not let us lose the conviction that it is only by supreme and superb exertions, unwearying and indomitable, that we shall save our souls alive. No one can predict, no one can even imagine, how this terrible war against German and Nazi aggression will run its course or how far it will spread or how long it will last. Long, dark months of trials and tribulations lie before us. Not only great dangers, but many more misfortunes, many shortcomings, many mistakes, many disappointments will surely be our lot. Death and sorrow will be the companions of our journey; hardship our garment; constancy and valour our only shield. We must be united, we must be undaunted, we must be inflexible. Our qualities and deeds must burn and glow through the gloom of Europe until they become the veritable beacon of its salvation.

8 October 1940

SHOWERS OF SPARKS AND BURNING EMBERS

To the layman, the fighting of a fire may appear a chaotic business. But beyond the incomprehensible maze of hose, beyond the roar of the pumps, the rivers of blackened water, the showers of sparks and burning embers, the hurrying and scurrying, lies a coldly calculated plan of action. This is no frantic improvization. Rather it is the application, to suit immediate circumstances, of a store of well-tried tactics and experience. Under the officer's helmet are thoughts of the wind, varied water pressures, draughts, building construction, high-explosive (H.E) damage to the structure of the building, difficulty of access to the building and reaching the seat of the fire, risk to his men from further collapse of masonry, risk to surrounding property, etc. Such knowledge and the intuition of experience will decide the tactics of his battle with the flames.

Below is the history of a fire. No two fires are quite alike: but this is a fair example of a reasonably typical case.

The building involved is an office-type building of fairly modern construction and large dimensions situated in a congested part of London. It consists of a basement with six storeys above. The topmost storey is contained within the roof.

At the centre of the building an ornamental clock tower rises to a further height of about 20 ft.

9.08pm	A shower of incendiaries, together with some high-explosive bombs fall in the vicinity of V ____ Street.
9.10pm	Reported by air raid warden that Messrs. J. & T.'s building in V ____ Street has been hit by H.E. and the roof is alight.
9.12pm	Trailer pump arrives at V ____ Street. Officer-in-charge sizes up the situation, observes that the roof and tower is seriously on fire, that the bomb explosion has demolished the west corner of the building and internal blast damage will make access to the upper floors very difficult, immediately sends back message for assistance.
	He calls for four additional pumps and a water tower.
	The pump's crew force an entry through the main doorway and, using a rope, haul the first line of hose up the stairwell. Pump operator outside has, in the meantime, connected his pump to a street hydrant and is ready to turn on the water.
9.15pm	Crew (A) have climbed to the topmost floor and find the fire is confined at present to the roof space and tower. Here is the first difficulty – water must be got on to the seat of the fire and access to roof spaces is usually restricted. A small traphatch fitted with a step-ladder is found and two men prepare to ascend with the branch.* A man is sent back to

---

* Technical term for hose nozzle

the pump with instructions for the pump operator to turn on the water. His instructions are precise: the pressure required has been calculated and he is informed of the position of the branchpipe.

The damaged western section has opened up the roof to the air and soon the entire roof is alight. It is evident that one jet is insufficient, and, leaving two men with the branch, the officer gets back to the pump with the remainder of his crew to lay out another line of hose.

9.25pm   Reinforcements of three trailer pumps and one heavy unit arrive. Two crews (B) and (C) are detailed to get to work on the floor immediately below roof 1 of the building involved. Their object is to check the downward progress of the fire.

It is apparent that the proximity and construction of other buildings constitutes a grave risk of the fire becoming a conflagration. A crew (D) is sent to roof 2 to direct a jet of water across the alleyway on to roof 1 and thence to the seat of the fire. The remaining crew (E) is sent to roof 3 for a similar purpose.

All access to roofs is made by internal stairs and lines of hose are hauled up outside the buildings.

Within a few minutes water is pumped through to each of these crews.

The officer's plan has been first to concentrate a strong jet of water at the seat of the fire, secondly to position branches in strategical positions in relation to the wind direction and possible spread of the fire to other buildings.

9.28pm   Enemy planes seem to have moved their main attack over this district. Possibly they are guided by the brilliant light of the fire. Bombs fall in the near vicinity and cause a further portion of the damaged buildings to collapse. None of the men are injured and the fighting of the fire continues without interruption.

Crew (A) finding their position in the roof space untenable have retreated to the floor below. The tremendous heat above causes the ceiling to split. Large pieces of plaster fall to the floor, causing minor cuts and bruises to the firemen.

9.30pm Now released of any restraining jet the fire spreads throughout the length of the roof. The clock tower, its supporting girders buckled by the heat and its fabric weakened by the shock of exploding high-explosive bombs, topples and falls inwards without warning. Crew (A) have no time to get clear. Two men, swept with tons of debris through several floors, are killed.

The officer immediately realizes that his chances of saving the building are small and that crews (B) and (C) are in risk of being cut off. He decides to withdraw them from the building.

A CHAIN OF BUCKETS

9.32pm

Water tower arrives and is set up at the western end of the building. Crew (B) connect their line of hose to the water tower. It is able to throw a strong jet on to the fire itself, and also on to the roof and windows of surrounding buildings.

Officer reviews situation, sends crew (C) to roof 2 to cover the eastern end of the building. A large body of fire was carried through the floors by the falling tower. Thus all floors are now involved.

Officer sends back message calling for five additional pumps and a second water tower. Also for a water relaying unit – since immediate supply from neighbouring hydrants will be insufficient to feed this added pump strength.

9.35pm

A senior officer and his staff arrive with a control car. The control point is set up and indicated with flashing lights.

A more detailed survey of the situation is now effected. It is found that all floors of the building are well alight and the roof is at the point of collapse. The building is too unsafe for crews to be permitted to work inside. It is decided to concentrate all efforts on confining the fire to the one building.

Additional pumps arrive and report to the control point. Here they are detailed where to position their jets and where to obtain water. Crews (F) and (G) are stationed at the entrances to the alleyways on either side of the fired building. These crews will throw a curtain of water covering the adjacent buildings (2) and (3) to combat any spread of fire in that direction.

Crews (H) and (K) are sent to the rear of the building to work from ground level.

9.40pm The second water tower arrives simultaneously with the water unit. The water tower is also positioned at the rear of the building and crew (K) connect their line of hose to it.

The water unit has laid twin lines of hose from a canal half a mile distant and the crew set up a canal reservoir in front of the building. This is speedily filled with water relayed from the canal. Three pumps (F), (G) and (J) get to work from this new water supply and crew (J) position their jet at the front of the building.

9.55pm The fire is now effectively surrounded. All jets are doing good work. The flames are prevented from spreading in any direction, the heavy volume of water is reducing the main body of fire. No further assistance will be required – the fire is on the point of being 'in hand'.

With these tactics, the fire is fought on through the night. From this point there is no further spread. It is now a matter of pouring more and ever more water on to salient points. The firemen attack relentlessly. As the intensity of the fire diminishes and daylight arrives they press home the attack and get to closer quarters, smashing home with their powerful jets of water until the flames are completely routed.

Next day The fire is out – but for embers and small pockets of fire among fallen wreckage. Firemen get down to the job of cooling the hot piles of ash and ember so that no light will be visible during black-out hours that night.

The danger is over – the building is badly damaged but the fire has been confined to reasonable limits and the neighbouring blocks have been saved.

ALL HANDS TO THE PUMP

The appliance specially recommended for dealing with incendiary bombs and the resultant fires is the stirrup hand-pump. It is fitted with a dual-purpose nozzle which can produce either a spray or an $\frac{1}{8}$ in. jet of water, as desired. It is supplied with 30 ft of hose. The jet will normally carry effectively to a range of about 30 ft, and the spray to about 15 ft.

Even when it is possible to do so, it would be unwise to attack a Magnesium (Electron) Bomb with the stirrup pump until it has been burning for about a minute, owing to the violence of the spluttering from the thermite core.

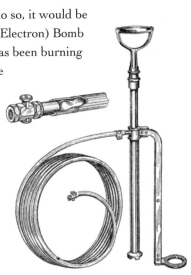

The advantage of the stirrup hand-pump may be summarized as follows:

(i)   It enables the fire to be fought from a safe distance, and away from the intense heat and smoke.

(ii)   It provides a means of attacking both the fire and the bomb, each of which requires separate treatment. To change from a jet to spray it is necessary only to press a button in the base of the nozzle.

(iii) It is economical in water consumption; 6 to 8 gallons of water should be sufficient to extinguish the bomb and any normal fire in a room in about five minutes.

(iv)   It is a valuable means of fighting incipient domestic fires not necessarily resulting from incendiary bombs.

METHOD OF USE

The pump may be operated efficiently by two people, but three are preferable, and each should undertake one of the following duties:

No. 1 takes charge of the fire-fighting and operates the nozzle at the end of the line of hose.

No. 2 pumps the water from a bucket at the other end of the hose.

No. 3 keeps the bucket replenished with water and relieves No. 2 as necessary.

He should also watch for the possible outbreak of fire in the floor below and in other likely places.

When the team consists of only two persons, the duties of No. 2 and No. 3 should be combined.

An independent source of water supply should be arranged in case water mains are damaged or the pressure of water in them is reduced owing to fire brigade activities elsewhere. For this purpose, water should be stored beforehand in tanks or buckets, or used bath water may be retained in the bath.

To approach the fire without being overcome by smoke, fumes, and heat, No. 1 of the team should lie down and keep his face near the floor where it will be found easier to breathe and to see. He should have an axe conveniently available for dealing with obstacles in his approach to the bomb and also an electric torch for use in the final search for smouldering remains. If a fireman's axe is not available, a light hatchet or crowbar may be used.

AN ALTERNATIVE METHOD

There is an alternative technique used in dealing with an incendiary bomb. In this, no attempt is made to accelerate the speed of burning of the bomb; the bomb is covered with dry sand or similar material and kept under control so that it may be safely scooped up and removed. This method cannot be employed when the bomb has caused a fire so extensive as to prevent a close approach to it being made, unless special protection can be provided. A wet blanket wrapped about the operator might offer some protection, but as this method does not readily lend itself to working in a prone position its uses are greatly restricted. This technique is also less appropriate where the bomb has fallen on a combustible surface through which it could quickly burn, and in general its use is recommended only where the bomb has fallen in surroundings not readily combustible or in the absence of a stirrup hand-pump and water.

USE OF CHEMICAL EXTINGUISHERS

Chemical extinguishers of the soda acid type, provided they are of sufficient capacity, would serve to deal with fire resulting from an incendiary bomb, but certain other types of chemical extinguishers designed for special purposes are dangerous and should not be used, since the chemicals contained in them will generate phosgene gas if brought into contact with burning magnesium.

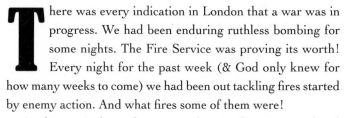

EAST END ABLAZE

F.W. Hurд, Fireman

There was every indication in London that a war was in progress. We had been enduring ruthless bombing for some nights. The Fire Service was proving its worth! Every night for the past week (& God only knew for how many weeks to come) we had been out tackling fires started by enemy action. And what fires some of them were!

On this particular night we turned out at about 9pm, ordered to Burdett Rd Fire Station. Well into the East End, & not <u>so</u> far from the river. Obviously, until we got there, there was no telling what was in store for us, so we were more or less prepared for anything. Just as well that we were. Arriving at Burdett Road, we could see that several large fires had got going & the whole area was illuminated by a ruddy glow. Fires started as we watched! Right opposite the fire-station a large church had just got hit. The roof burst into flame as I dismounted from my pump to report my arrival & by the time I had crossed the road the whole lot was well alight. The 'Red' pump turned out as I entered the station. Inside the Control Room the mobilizing staff were almost overwhelmed with calls. Some to fires already burning & requiring more assistance, but the majority from Wardens & Police to fires just started. I 'take off my hat' to the

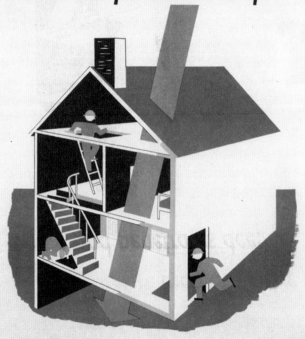

Watchroom staffs, men & women. <u>They</u> are the people to thank for getting fires attended as soon as they break out. When a big raid is in progress they are hard at it, often all night, under pretty tough conditions.

At Burdett Rd the sole illumination was a candle beside each telephone operator, the Mobilizing Officer & his assistant. The room was full of 'No 1' (man in charge) men reporting as I was. No sooner had we given the necessary information (Station coming from, type of appliance, number of men in crew & name of man in charge) than we were dispatched off to fires. My pump was ordered to proceed in convoy with 4 others to an area in which were about three major fires in progress. The senior man of the convoy reported to the Officer in charge of the fires & we were sent (still in convoy) somewhere about ½ mile from the fire & to start 'series pumping', getting our supply from a canal. Now, it's no joke finding your way about in a vehicle during the black-out through back-streets in a district you or your driver have never been in before! As we were now some distance away from the fires & Jerry being overhead we were proceeding without lights (except for side-lights, which are so dimmed as to be useless for illuminating the road). The pump in front of us had turned round a corner. We followed, & suddenly the tender bumped & lurched & went along with two wheels on the pavement. My driver swore, then said something about the men who were supposed to put road lamps around. We had only just missed dropping into a crater about 20 ft across by 10–15 ft deep. We stopped & I got out to see whether we could proceed or not. What a mess! The first pump (a heavy unit) had swerved the other way to us, & was stuck with its nose in a heap of debris. Then a Warden came up, showed us a way past the crater &, in answer to my rather (I'm afraid) terse & blunt enquiry as to why there were no so & so lamps around the blank hole said, rather apologetically, 'I'm sorry mate, but that there 'ole only happened about 5 minutes ago!' I apologized, we straightened out the convoy, extricated the H.U. [heavy unit] & eventually got to our destination.

We positioned our pumps ready for series working, but there was a house burning alongside my pump so we put that out first. It didn't take long. Of all the monotonous jobs, I think series pumping is the worst. The idea is to relay water from a considerable distance either direct or, as in this case, to [a] point adjacent to the fire. Pumps are spaced about 1000 ft apart, starting from the water supply, & water is pumped through this 'chain', each pump passing the water on. The pumps are used to maintain pressure, as over long distances the 'lifting' pump is not sufficient to force the water thro'. We were, as I have said, at least ½ mile from the fire & there was nothing for my crew to do except keep an eye on the line of hose occasionally. We walked round & saw that the street we were in had already been devastated by previous raids. All the houses were evacuated, & not one of them was intact! (This street connected two other streets which ran across the top & bottom of the road I was in.) In the top street a row of shops had their fronts blown away, &, such is the peculiarity of 'blast', although most of the actual front had gone, bunches of bananas, jars of jam etc., were still in place on the shelves behind. While we were looking at this phenomenon, I saw something chalked on a door, & got quite a shock when I read 'Police Notice, Unexploded inside this shop'. We didn't stay there long.

During this time the raider had near left the vicinity, & as the A.A. [ack-ack] guns were rather active we had quite a lot of shrapnel around. We had heard at frequent intervals bombs falling, but they didn't come near us. Then, suddenly, I heard

LIGHT TRAILER FIRE-PUMP IN ACTION

'something' coming my way. I ducked! Laid flat under a pump. Just as I flopped down a terrific burst of flame lit up the sky & I could see a large fire suddenly appear about ¼ mile away. But still this 'thing' kept coming down. 'It' was an oil bomb & it landed in the middle of a factory at the bottom of the road. Not 200 yds away, if that. The whole place just went up in one sheet of flame.

As soon as it happened, the supply pump 'knocked off' (it was about 400 yds the other side of the factory) & I ordered my pump down to the fire. But by the time I had got there (about 3 minutes after the bomb) I saw that there was nothing I could do as there were already 2 pumps there at work. There was not sufficient water to supply more. I took my pump back up the road, collected my hose (series pumping was not resumed) and decided to find cover, it being foolhardy to keep exposed unnecessarily. We had been pumping into a dam about 100 yds along the top road inside a school yard. Pulling up outside the school, I went in the yard & found there two Anderson Shelters. These already had about a dozen chaps in them, the crews of the other 'series' pumps. I went back to the pump to collect my crew, when we heard some more stuff coming close. We all ducked, there was a terrific explosion, the appliance jumped & rocked, the round 'came up & hit me'. 3 H.E. [High Explosive] bombs had dropped in the road I had just left!

It was now about 3 o/c in the morning. We seemed to have been forgotten by everybody, as no Officer came near us, nor did we receive any orders. We stayed in or close to that shelter till about 4.30, as it was still pretty thick outside. A little while later it eased off & another chap (in charge of a pump from my own station) & myself decided we'd take our pumps & see what we could do. Anything being better than staying still there. Just as we were leaving, a Fireman came along & told us we were to go back to Burdett Rd Stn. We found our way back after a bit. It was awkward, for a lot of the road we had previously travelled had been bombed. Pumps were still being sent out from the station to other fires! As we had been at work all night, we were not sent out immediately. Some hero had made tea! Did it taste good. The 'All Clear' went about 6 o/c. As soon as they received the message that most fires were under control the pumps from farthest away were ordered home. I was one of them. But what a journey I had to get back. It took two hours! That night the enemy 'did' the city. Fires were still raging. Cheapside was alight amost along one side. Still, we made it. Got home about 8.15am. The leave men returned to duty at 9am & they were out almost right away on relief crews.

That certainly was some night! Some of our crews nearer to the actual fires than I was actually went from building to building putting out fires as they started. It was really heart-breaking. No sooner would a fire be 'got under' than it would be hit & start off again, or else one would be started next door to it. I know what it is to feel really tired nowadays!!

'THE THINGUMMY-BOB'

David Heneker

You've heard of Florence Nightingale, Grace Darling and
    the rest
You've all seen Greta Garbo and our bosom friend Mae West
But there's a little lady I want you all to meet
She's working on munitions and she lives just down the street.
She can't pretend to be a great celebrity
But still she's most important in her way
The job she has to do may not sound much to you
But all the same I'm very proud to say.

She's the girl that makes the thing
That drills the hole that holds the spring
That drives the rod that turns the knob
That works the thingummy-bob.
She's the girl that makes the thing
That holds the oil that oils the ring
That takes the shank that moves the crank
That works the thingummy-bob.
It's a ticklish sort of job making a thing for a thingummy-bob
Especially when you don't know what it's for.
But it's the girl that makes the thing

A young woman places the gramophone needle on a record to bring some light relief to an air raid shelter, somewhere in north London.

That drills the hole that holds the spring
That works the tingummy-bob that makes the engine roar
But it's the girl that makes the thing
That holds the oil that oils the ring
That makes the thingummy-bob that's going to win the war.

She's not what you would call a heroine at all
I don't suppose you'll ever hear her name
But though she'll never boast of her important post
She strikes a blow for freedom just the same.

THE TON BOMB

John Strachey, Air Raid Warden

At five minutes to seven on a Friday evening Ford was getting into his overalls when the Blitz began, noisily. […] He began to walk down James Street. Immediately he was in another world. People were moving about and coming up. He saw that the houses opposite him were very considerably shattered. He looked farther down the street and saw that there were no houses. […]

Before he had got opposite to the part of James Street that did not appear to be there, he met Miss Sterling. She pointed at the shattered-looking but still standing houses and said, 'There's a good many people in there.' Mrs Morley came up, smooth and undisturbed. She said, 'The mobile unit' (a sort of medical advance guard consisting of doctor, nurse, and stretcher-bearers) 'has just gone in there,' pointing to No. 50.

Ford went into this house. The ground- and first-floor rooms were more or less all right – nothing more than blown out window frames and shattered plaster. But up from the first floor the stairs were ankle deep in rubble. He went up, passing the second-floor rooms. The two top-floor rooms and the top landing were deeply encumbered with debris, rubble, slates and roof timber. He looked up; there was no roof overhead. There were dark clouds, picked out with momentary sparkles of shell bursts, reflected gun flashes and an uneasy searchlight waving its futility.

In the first room two men of a stretcher party, a nurse and another man were bending over a figure lying on a heap of the plaster rubble. Ford saw that it was an injured man. His breathing was violent and laboured. They seemed to be trying to get something down his throat through some sort of tube. One of the stretcher-bearers saw Ford. Pointing to the back room he said, 'There are two more in there.' Ford looked in, cautiously using his torch, supplementing its metal hood with his hand. This room was wrecked. One side of it was heaped halfway up to the ceiling with debris. Several roof timbers lay across it. Ford began to clamber his way into it. He saw something dark lying at his feet. He put the beam of his torch on it and saw that it was a girl. [...]

Ford hadn't much doubt that she was dead. She looked so small for one thing; and there was a severe head wound. But he wondered what could have caused fatal injuries. The roof timbers were fairly light and had only a few feet to fall. With a feeling of intimacy, he took up her unresisting hand and felt for a pulse. To his surprise he felt, or thought he felt, a very feeble beat. He went back to the front room and said, 'Is there a doctor here?' One of the stretcher party said, 'He's a doctor, but he's busy.' He pointed at an oldish man bending over the other casualty. Ford said, 'I think the girl in here is alive. Will you come and see?' The doctor gave no sign of having heard. But after a time he came. He ran a hypodermic into the grey, debris-encrusted flesh of her arm – 'just in case,' he said. He felt for the pulse, but said, 'Very improbable.' – 'Where's the injury?' said the doctor. Ford said, 'Her head, I think.' – 'The *head?*' said the doctor, as if astonished. Then he ran his fingers over her skull, under her blood and rubble-matted hair. But he said

Auxiliary Fireman Brian Montagnol Gilks carries a casualty over his shoulders as he leaves a bomb-damaged building during a 'shout' somewhere in London.

nothing. Ford said, 'Shall I take her downstairs?' The doctor said, 'No.' So they left her, lying easily on the debris, looking through the roof at the sky.

When Ford got back to the street he found that Strong had taken over as 'incident officer', and got the two masked, light-blue lamps burning to mark his position. This is an excellent arrangement by which a light-blue flag is hung out by day and light-blue lamps are lighted at night, to mark the spot where stands the incident officer. The incident officer is responsible for co-ordinating the work of the wardens, the rescue squads, the stretcher parties, the ambulances, and the AFS units (if there is fire). [...]

He found Tyne, radiating competence and confidence, with Strong. Someone came up with a written message (all messages, and this also has proved a correct arrangement, are sent in writing even over a distance of a few hundred yards whenever possible). Strong said, 'More wardens are wanted at Lothian Cottages. Will you both go there, please?'. [...]

Ford began to be able to see that here, too, a number of houses had been demolished; and a good many of those still standing were well shattered. He supposed vaguely that this was the result of another bomb, falling close to the one which had evidently come down in James Street. He began climbing across the debris-covered area. He went about 20 yds, not without difficulty. The darkness seemed even thicker here; no doubt there was more unsettled dust. He found half a dozen or so rescue men digging hard at a mound. [...]

The cries and groans went on unnervingly from underneath. Ford began to distinguish one woman's voice saying, 'Oh, my God, we're done for – I know we are – I know we are. – Why don't you come?' Then he noticed a figure which seemed to be neither a rescue man nor a warden, nor a stretcher-bearer. This figure was moving about uneasily in order to avoid the stream of flying bricks that they were throwing backwards through their legs. The figure began to talk to whoever was in the mound. It said, 'That's quite all right, Mrs Wells. Now *don't* become frightened. We're getting to you *very* rapidly. There is *no* cause for alarm. All will be well.' Ford felt certain it must be the Vicar; it was. [...]

Every now and then the gunfire would get heavier, and they would hear an enemy 'plane, apparently directly overhead. Then the rescue men would all shout 'Lights – put that light out', and insist on every torch, even the most carefully masked, being put out, so that they had to work on in total blackness. The rescue men were extremely fussy and particular about this. An hour of labour, scrabbing in the gritty rubble and brickwork, now turning slimy in the rain, went by. About every ten minutes the rescue men would shout for silence. Everyone would stop dead. The rescue men who had burrowed deepest would ask for the buried people to give their position. Ford found these silences eerie.

At first there seemed to be two other voices as well as Mrs Wells'. But the last time there was only one other voice. Gradually the outlines of an unshattered floor, the boards still holding to the joists, began to be revealed in the mound. They all guessed at once that this floor must be held up, if only a foot or so, by something. Only this could account for the fact that there were people alive underneath. For there were many tons of debris on top. Human beings could only have survived if at least one end of this floor was being held up off them, so that a sort of tiny lean-to had been formed. They dug on, trying to reveal the general contours of whatever trace of structure must be there. Before they had succeeded, Ford and the two rescue men working next to him abruptly uncovered a man's leg. It stuck out of the debris from the knee down. This leg gave one convulsive kick or twitch and then hung still. It would have been quite useless to attempt to pull on it, since the body to which it was attached was deeply buried. So all they could do was to go on digging, in general round the leg, but more with reference to the still audible voice than to it.

Gradually the chance-built construction which had kept the buried voices alive became evident. They had unearthed the edge of the unbroken floor along 10 ft or so of its length. And, sure enough, a very low cave – not more than 6 to 9 in. high, could be detected under about half its length. A rescue man who appeared to be leading this squad called out 'Jacks'. A couple of men began clambering back over the debris and after a bit came back with two short, strong jacks and some wooden blocks. For some time it was impossible to get a jack, even when fully closed, under the uncovered floor joists. But by means of scrabbing debris from under it this was finally done. Then the jack was cranked open. One corner of the floor shifted a few inches downwards. They got blocks under it and, with some trouble, shifted the jack along. They began to raise the floor a little farther. But now the base of the jack itself kept slipping and giving in the shifting debris. The floor rose an inch or so, only to fall back onto the blocks. The rescue men began to feel baffled. The soaking rain was turning the rubble into a disgusting gritty paste which covered them from head to foot. The droning overhead never ceased. One of the rescue men said, 'Can't do nothing here – let's go.' Another said, 'Shut up, you bloody bastard, they'll hear you.'

Apparently the suggestion of giving up had not been serious, because no one took any further notice of it. They all began digging with their hands again, hoping to find a new point of

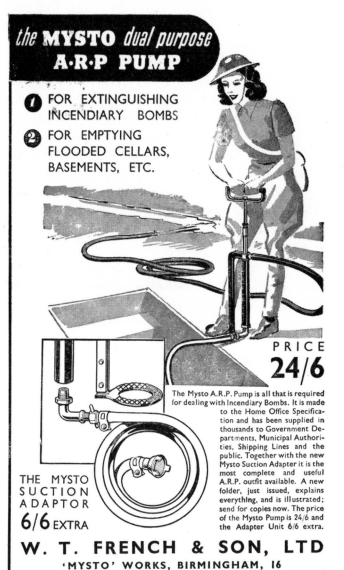

attack from which the floor could be raised. Mrs Wells began groaning and crying out again. At any rate it showed them where she was. [...]

The rescue men at the far end seemed to be making progress. They had got the jack into action again and raised the floor several inches. They had succeeded in getting several new blocks into place. The rescue man next to Ford said, 'We could get a prop under here.' Ford went off to look for a stout bit of debris. He found it almost immediately and came back with it. 'Not wanted,' he was told. 'They're out.' Ford saw with amazement that in the, say, 150 seconds he had been away the whole scene had been transformed. The floor had evidently been raised just sufficiently to take all pressure off the buried persons. Two women had either crawled or been pulled out, and there they were on the two stretchers that had been lying waiting for them. The stretcher-bearers were giving them cups of tea out of a thermos. Both women seemed quite all right, and were talking excitedly. The stretcher-bearers picked them up, carried them laboriously over the debris, and out through the entrance into Leavon Street. [...]

By seven o'clock it was light. Ford climbed up to the rim of the crater again. It was not till then that he got a clear grasp of what had really happened. Now he saw that all the damage had been done by one very large bomb which had landed perhaps 2 ft from the back of the houses on this side of James Street. (The official report stated that it was almost certainly of the one-ton category, the largest standard size dropped by the Germans on London.) It had fallen directly upon several Anderson Shelters which had been built in their backyards. The crater itself was some hundred feet across, and about 30 ft deep, measuring from the top of the rim of the debris, which was itself between 10 and 15 ft above street level. For perhaps another 20 yds from the rim of the crater everything had been levelled to the ground. Beyond that the houses, although shattered, still stood. Many of them, as Ford had found on his night clamber across the devastated area, had debris piled against them, up to the level of their first-floor windows. It looked as if they had been washed by some night tide bearing on it the remains of distorted ships, rocks and sea growths.

The official summary of damage subsequently showed that, in all, nine houses had been totally demolished and eighteen more so badly damaged that they would have to be pulled down.

'ONE ENORMOUS HOLE'

Herbert Brush

The worst night yet. After a day of continual alarms I had just gone to sleep when about 10.30pm the dug-out rocked all ways at once and I thought that our last hours had come this time. I came out of the dug-out expecting I don't know what, but the house still stood. There was a bright light in the road and I soon found out that it was an incendiary burning near the fence next door, so I took a bucket of water which was standing ready and my home-made stirrup pump and hurried to the fire, which was caused by one of those beastly oil-bombs. I and a warden soon put out the blaze with the spray and then there was time to look round.

A fire at the bottom end of Kirkdale had started and was gradually getting brighter until the flames lit up the whole district and we expected that Jerry would soon be back with a fresh supply of bombs. The shaking of the dug-out was accounted for by a bomb which had fallen in Thorpewood Avenue about 200 yds away. This bomb had made a huge hole in the road and cut one house clean in two, and seriously damaged several others. We were lucky to escape with no damage as far as I can see. The shaking stopped all the clocks in the house, one an electric clock which has run off a battery for

WHAT THE HOUSEHOLDER CAN DO TO MEET THE DANGERS THREATENED BY AIR RAIDS : PRECAUTIONS AGAINST HIGH EXPLOSIVE AND GAS ; AND THE METHOD OF DEALING WITH INCENDIARY BOMBS.

months without attention. Sticky oil is all over the road this morning and if it gets on one's shoes it takes a long time to get off. If that bomb had fallen on the house nothing could have saved the place, with all that oil on the rafters and furniture. Luckily for us it fell in the road about 40 yds away from the house in a straight line, and sprayed the oil all over the fences and footway and across the road. The PO pillar-box where we generally post our letters is now black instead of red; it was within 10 yds of the oil-bomb. I noticed when the postman was clearing the letters that none of the stuff had gone through the slot. It took me a long time to clean the oil off the rubber hose and pump and off the soles of my shoes, but I have still got the smell of the stuff in my nose.

3pm W and I went round to look at the allotment, but it was a case of looking *for* the allotment. Four perches out of the five are one enormous hole and all my potatoes and cabbages have vanished. Apparently the bomb fell on the footpath between two allotments and when it exploded had preference for mine, although I must say that there is not much left of Hardy's, and the plot on the other side of mine has a huge pile of my earth on it. The result is that all my work there has been wasted, absolutely wasted, and the potatoes at Christmas certainly will not come off my allotment, though if I have sufficient energy for some deep excavations I may find a potato or two somewhere in the mountain on each side of the 10-ft hole. When I went there the other day I noticed that there were several nice cabbages nearly ready to eat, and I meant to dig potatoes this weekend. Now I should have some difficulty in finding the place where they stood.

26 October 1940, London

'LAST WORDS'

A.P. Herbert

When I am not escaping from
The blast of some gigantic bomb,
It seems I have to listen to
A list of things that threatened you.
And it is odd how full of fun
And interest I find the one,
But what intolerable bores
Are almost any bombs of yours.

I wish that I could make you see
The *kind* of thing that just missed me.
It wasn't, by the best report,
The 'aerial torpedo' sort;
Nor yet that monster of the sky
Men call a 'land-mine' – Lord knows why –
Though in some ways quite like the two:
No, this, I think, was something *new*.
For size? Well, you have seen a whale –
Say, sixty yards, from head to tail:
And, as for depth, well, I suppose
A large giraffe, from top to toes.

Well, this thing whistled through my hair
And quite destroyed St Peter's Square.
It passed, I say, it passed my brow
As close as you are sitting now;
And Numbers One to Seventeen
Might just as well have never been;
While there was nothing much to see
Of Twenty-one to Fifty-three.
I had, you know, a mole upon
My forehead. Well, the mole has gone.
And Mrs Foster's garden gate
Is on the roof of Number Eight.
Imagine, if you can, the sound
Before this horror hit the ground!
You talk of 'whistles'. This was more
Like twenty-seven lions' roar;
Or shall we say ten twelve-inch shells
All whizzing down enormous wells.
It took about an hour to fall;
I was collected through it all:
Indeed, I made a will and got
It witnessed while the bomb was hot.

Now you. You say a big one fell
Close to the shrubbery? Oh, well –
No doubt it *seemed* a little near,
But things aren't *quite* what they appear.
'*That* was a close one', people say,
When really it was MILES away.
Apart from that, it's hard to tell
If it's a bomb or just a shell.

AFS Van with recruitment advert, 1940s.

Maybe a dud. It sounds to me
Like one of ours – a 1.3.

And anyhow, you must admit
The chance is small of being *hit*.
Why, London is the strangest place.
Nine-tenths of it is open space.
So think, when you are in a room,
It's nine times safer than the tomb.
And if this reassuring thought
Does not assure you, well it ought.

No, do not duck. And *never* run.
Don't be so silly. That's a gun.

23 October 1940

COVENTRY, 14 NOVEMBER 1940

Margaret Chifney and G.A. Hollingsworth

My second visit [to Coventry] I made with the other land girls and some soldiers from a local unit, to a dance in the YMCA, we went in an army lorry. After about an hour the air raid warning went but no one seemed to be worried, we were told they don't come this far, <u>they</u> being the German planes. The next few minutes had the man eating his words for tonight they had got this far and had come in force, and to stay. […]

The warden was trying to get us all out of the building which was well alight by now but when we got outside every building seemed to be on fire and in the distance flames were lighting up the Cathedral. I was petrified and couldn't move. A warden dragged me to the ground as the scream of another bomb came, but he left me to run to a woman who was on fire, he rolled her on the ground to put the flames out and took her to a shelter. I looked around to see if I could see any of the girls I had come with, but more bombs were falling and I needed somewhere to shelter. The moon was like a huge torchlight and the road[s] had ice on them, the trees were sparkling with the frost. I heard another screaming bomb and threw myself behind a hedge and a short wall and covered my ears against the bang. I don't know how long I stayed, it seemed like hours. There were so many buildings burning now the firemen were helping people rather than trying to put the fires out, it was impossible.

I knew if I didn't move soon, I would die of the cold, how I wished I had my old breeches and boots on instead of a dress and these silly shoes, how could I run in those? I tried to get an idea which way the station was. I thought if I got there I may be able to get back to base, so I got up and started to walk and then run a little in the direction of the railway. When I looked up in the bright moonlight I saw a parachute with what looked like a dustbin lid on it, so I found another wall to hide behind. I lay there, covered my ears and waited, but the explosion did not come so I had another try for the station. I went up the wrong road twice and found myself almost back in the town when I recognized a black building that I knew was on the way to the station.

After what seemed like hours I saw the railway bridge and I thought, at last, and then for the second time that night I was dragged to the ground, this time by a fireman. He said something and pointed to the railway and hanging there like a chandelier was the land mind, the parachute was caught on the bridge.

I spent the rest of the night wet, cold and very frightened in a lady's coal cellar under her house. There were several other occupants, one poor lady had completely lost her mind. She was screaming and trying to get out, saying her son was in the city, it was unbelievable.

How I got back is still a mystery. I had a ride in a car and tractor and the last transport I remember was a horse and cart, but the welcome I got when I did arrive helped me to recover. I was so happy to see they were all safe, they thought I had been trapped in the building. I just collapsed in a heap and cried myself to sleep. […]

When I returned to Coventry two weeks later to go home on leave there was nothing I could recognize, even the Cathedral had only half one spire left, it was heartbreaking. I am pleased that the new Cathedral has included some of the ruins, this way no one will ever forget, so many heroes, police, wardens, firemen, and most people who were not burnt themselves helped those who were burnt, it amazes me that anyone came out of there alive.

Margaret Chifney

14 [November] Thursday
Murderous 11 hour smashing air attack on Cov. 1000's casualties. 5 police killed by 1 bomb. Centre of town absolutely demolished. Hospitals, churches, shelters, ARP centres flattened, cathedral destroyed. 1000's homeless. No water, gas, electricity or food.

15 Friday
Biked to Kenilworth for this night after tortuous ordeal. No milk. Delayed actions all over burning city. King & Queen visit Coventry remains. Morrison & MP came to stare. Out of 500 planes, marvellous overwhelming total of 2 shot down.

16 Saturday
Must have been an accident. It was terrific. We escaped with shattered windows & leaking roof. Ambulances from B'ham, London & USA, fire engines & rescue workers from every corner of Britain also. Went to get wages. Then to Simms at night. The memory of this will last for ever in every citizen's mind. Places still burning. Soldiers digging for bodies. Hundreds crowding round Council House, which is still standing, to get news of missing relatives.

A Union Flag hangs defiantly from a building in the aftermath of the air raid which devastated the centre of Coventry on the night of 14/15 November 1940.

17 Sunday

Coventry attack front page news in New York. Stayed at Simms. City's walls which still stand are being dynamited to stop risk of further fires and falling masonry, explosions all day. Mobile canteens round town. DAs [Delayed Action bombs] still being found & also exploding.

18 Monday

2 killed at Humber on digging them out. 1000's Irish soldiers arriving all day to fill craters & dead bodies still being disinterred from the graves made by the Germans. DA in Stoke Park not yet exploded.

19 Tuesday

Still no water. Smells all over town horrid. 5,000 school children gone to Nuneaton, Kenilworth & Warwick, Stratford & Leamington. People sleep on streets, & many in cowsheds. Ken slightly bombed last night.

20 Wednesday

172 victims buried in mass funeral yesterday. Coffins covered by Union Jack. 1000's mourners. Craters gradually being filled in.

G.A. Hollingsworth

EVERYTHING SEEMED TO BE BURNING...

E.A. Platt

During November the long raid on Coventry brought us back with a big jolt! It was so near to us that everyone began to expect further action very shortly on our own patch again.

Once more we were under attack on three out of four nights – and this only four days after 'Coventrated' came into our dictionary. […]

This was possibly the worst raid of all, up to that time, and although the regulars [at the dance hall] danced until the close 'and the band played on', it was obvious to all that there was heavy damage and a large number of casualties being caused. […]

The long walk home that night was unforgettable… I walked for about three hours, and it was 2am when I arrived at my destination. The centre of the city was literally on fire – it was reminiscent of old 'Chicago' – arcades, shops, multiple stores – everything seemed to be burning, except the Cathedral!

I have two vivid memories of that walk – one is of consistently treading on broken glass – and the other of the number of people walking about with bundles of clothes and suitcases, just like the

A pile of girders, timber and rubble is all that is left of a building on the corner of George Street and Hospital Street in Birmingham, November 1940.

films of D.Ps after the end of the war! These people were possibly on their way to rest centres after being bombed out of their homes.

[...] Two ARP ambulances and rescue squads were in the road – and near to our house. I noted the one opposite (house) was in ruins. Ours was still there, but no windows and two very heavy front doors plus a tree were strewn in front of it.

I stood outside – transfixed(?) – petrified(?) – and didn't move from the spot until I lit and smoked a cigarette.

I then approached a Warden and asked him if there was anyone in the ambulances from No. 36 – amidst thoughts of spending the rest of the night visiting wards in casualty hospitals – the victims that could speak said 'no' – the warden checked with other rescue workers, and found that no one had been inside.

He led the way with the torch – and standing on the front and hall doors – with keys in hand – I said 'I think I'd better go first because I have all the keys!' Fortunately, Dad and Step-Mother were OK, in the room at the rear. Activity had been that heavy that the neighbours asked them to join them in their shelter.

After the long walk and subsequent shock, I was quite thirsty – so I made myself a cup of luke-warm cocoa – with a kettle on the dying embers of the fire (in the grate!). It tasted of brick-dust – that's reasonable – as everything was covered in it, but it's the finest drink I've ever had. The french windows in the room were shattered, and I remember getting sleep during the rest of the night broken by the violent flashes of bombs and anti-aircraft fire.

Only one brick had come out of the wall – and it was a central one – which landed midway on my bed. The front room was devastated – apart from one full pint of milk which remained unbroken!

Birmingham

BOMBED BUT STILL CARRYING ON

Vera Brittain

As we drive north over Tower Bridge towards Whitechapel and Shoreditch, the customary banshee note of the siren reverberates loudly from the river. We are looking with interest at the scattering of small debris round the Tower and the marks of attack on the walls of the Royal Mint, when a steel-helmeted policeman stops our car.

'It is my duty,' he announces solemnly, 'to warn you that an air raid alarm has sounded.'

Our Cockney owner-driver throws him a glance of unutterable contempt.

'Which way's Bethnal Green?' he inquires laconically.

'Two and a half miles to the left,' responds the policeman, his obligation as guardian of the reckless public which persists in driving through air raids now punctually fulfilled. Our chauffeur, we learn later, sleeps imperturbably on the top floor of a small block of Kennington flats which owns no shelter. Aerial torpedoes and high explosive bombs go off nightly around him without disturbing his poise. Towards the end of the day, showing us the gruesome remains of an entire street wiped out by a huge bomb which fell in the grounds of the Imperial War

A family's refuge-room with a Morrison shelter in it which doubles as a games table.

Museum a few hundred yards from his flat, his voice rings with the satisfaction of an Ancient Mariner describing his particular Battle of Trafalgar.

'Got on me toes when I heard that one, I did!' he tells us. 'Went out to find it, and was there before the ARP crowd themselves!'

He goes on to give us grisly details of casualties dug out by a detachment of troops from the wreckage of surface shelters destroyed by a direct hit in his neighbourhood. The possibility of becoming, in some future raid, another such casualty appears to disturb him not at all.

'Unless it has me name on it, it won't git me,' he affirms, typical of the fatalistic Londoner in his belief that destiny remains unaffected by caution. The numerous 'crumps' which have occurred in his district inspire him with pride rather than apprehension, and he repudiates firmly the suggestion that any other London borough might have produced a longer roll of casualties than his.

We drive on through the air raid down Whitechapel Road. The appearance of the Mile End Road, into which we run after negotiating a huge smash where the two thoroughfares join, suggests that not one London raid could have occurred without a bomb or two dropping directly upon it; but this morning the wrecked street remains quiet, and we hear no warning explosive sounds. As we reach Bow from Stepney and Whitechapel, I reflect lugubriously on the similarity of debris wherever it is found. Whether the crashed building stood in Bow Road or in Berkeley Square, its damp, blackened ruins equally suggest that nothing worth saving was kept in the house.

At a corner close to Bow Road Station, the wreckage of a Mission Hall wears a conspicuous placard:

'BOMBED BUT STILL CARRYING ON.'

We notice with relief that, though the famous bells are silenced, the small architectural jewel which is Bow Church still faces undamaged the wide tragic street with the gentle innocence of a nursery rhyme invented in a kinder and simpler age. A hundred yards or so farther on, a wide area of industrial ruin barely concealed by hurriedly erected hoardings is marked – with intentional humour? we wonder – by a large rough notice-board:

'THIS FREEHOLD SITE
FOR DISPOSAL.'

YOUR COURAGE

YOUR CHEERFULNESS

YOUR RESOLUTION

WILL BRING

US VICTORY

On the other side of Bow Bridge over the River Lee, the car suddenly reaches a square half-mile of devastation so complete that even our damage-accustomed eyes examine it with a fixed stare of incredulity. All life, all semblance of human habitation, has disappeared from these crushed and flattened acres; the place is a No Man's Land, an Aceldama, a burnt and blackened Limbo containing the foul rubbish of an exploded civilization.

The driver, his comprehensive knowledge of London defeated by the sinister metamorphosis, beckons one of the khaki-uniformed members of the Auxiliary Military Pioneers who are digging among the ruins.

'Where's this?' he inquires peremptorily.

'Old Ford Road,' briefly replies the conscripted student of East End archaeology. A moment later, we pass a railway station, still hopefully announcing 'Trains to all parts'. Beyond the station, the surviving skeleton of a former wall is labelled with equal optimism: 'Factory Premises to Let.' As we run into Bethnal Green, the pile of debris that confronts us provokes even our imperturbable driver to comment.

'That was a naughty one!' he murmurs, a suspicion of wry amusement mingled even with his evident sympathy for those fellow-Cockneys who have suffered such severe devastation. Instinctively I look into the sky to see whether any more 'naughty ones' are preparing to demolish the car, but I perceive only the barrage balloons, swinging like white iridescent pearls against the pale cobalt-blue sky. I am still tentatively regarding them, when the steady booming note of the 'All Clear' assures me that someone else's air raid is over.

ENCOUNTERING THE ENEMY

Home Guard Manual

PATROLS

There are three types of patrols: –

    (a)   Reconnoitring patrols.

    (b)   Fighting patrols.

    (c)   Standing patrols.

RECONNOITRING PATROLS

(i) **Reconnoitring patrols** may be sent out on either –

    (a)   Reconnaissance for purposes of protection to give warning of the presence of the enemy, e.g., sent out from outposts before dawn to discover if the enemy have worked up close to positions during the night.

    (b)   Special reconnaissance, as for example, gaining information about enemy defences, reconnoitring lines of advance, etc.

    Strength, usually one section.

(ii) **Orders:** The success of a patrol depends on the leader. Before going out he will receive orders including: –

(a)   What is known of the enemy.

(b)   Position of forward detachments of our own troops.

(c)   The object of the patrol (straightforward questions to be asked: 'Is there any enemy in HALL FARM?')

(d)   When patrol is to go out, and when return.

(e)   Route to be followed.

(f)   Password.

(g)   Whether bodies of our own troops have been notified that patrol is going out.

(iii) **Preparations** before setting out: –

(a)   Reconnaissance: Leader should study the ground, noting landmarks and aids to keeping direction at night, bounds, obstacles, observation points. He will then make his plan.

(b)   He will see that every man knows the orders so that if he becomes a casualty the patrol can carry on.

(c)   Patrol to go out lightly equipped: rifles and few extra rounds only.

(d)   Patrol to move silently at night, see equipment does not rattle.

(e)   No letters, papers, maps to be taken on patrol.

(iv) **The Route:** This is decided by the officer who sends the patrol out, but it is a general route only. The patrol leader must carefully plan his exact route. Do not use the same route twice.

(v) **The Approach** to an objective is to be planned by the patrol leader. He is to get information without fighting. It is better to approach from the rear or a flank. Do not do the obvious. Advance will usually be by bounds from cover to cover. Make provision for protection against surprise, and method of getting information back if the patrol is wiped out. This may be done by the use of scouts and get-away men.

The distances between scouts, patrol and get-away men will depend on the ground and visibility. Must always keep patrol in view.

(vi) **Withdrawing** the patrol will still be by bounds, a portion of patrol withdrawing to next position in rear from which they can cover the withdrawal of the remainder of the patrol.

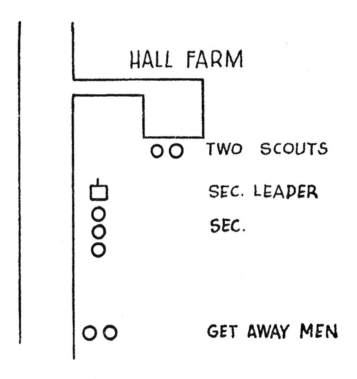

(vii) **By night,** it is best not to move by bounds, but at a steady pace with frequent halts. Silence is essential. If a surprise collision with enemy takes place, it is best to go straight in before he has time to collect his wits. Keep to low ground by night, use shadow as much as possible.

In all circumstances patrol leaders will use their initiative and modify any of the above to suit existing conditions.

FIGHTING PATROLS

(i) Fighting patrols are usually at least one platoon sent out under an officer. They carry full equipment and weapons, and are sent out to act as covering parties in defence, to delay the enemy during a withdrawal, to harass the enemy, or to secure identifications. They must be prepared to act offensively.

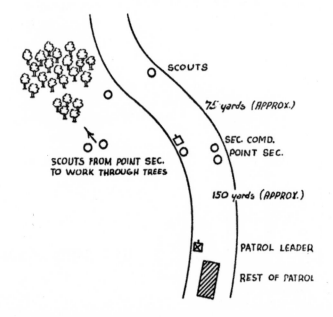

(ii) **Formations** adopted should be such as will give maximum protection to front and flanks. When not in close contact with the enemy, and moving along a road, the patrol may have a point section forward, with scouts to watch either flank. If in closer contact with the enemy, a more open formation must be adopted. The position of the patrol commander to be where he can best command his patrol (usually well forward). Distances between sections will depend on the ground.

(iii) **Advancing:** When enemy is encountered, patrol advances by bounds from feature to feature. The leader selects a position, and the forward section advances to it under cover of fire (if necessary) from the remainder of the patrol. On gaining the position, this section then covers the advance of the remainder of the patrol to the position. Positions selected should have a good field of fire. In approaching a building, bridge, etc., thought to be occupied, it should be well covered by the patrol while scouts advance to investigate.

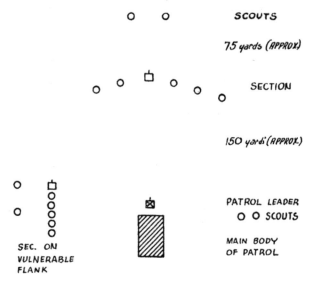

(iv) **Withdrawing** will be on similar lines, i.e., bounds from position to position.

(v) **By night** the best formation to adopt will depend on the darkness of the night, distance from the enemy, nature of the ground, etc. Usually patrols will have to move in closer formation than by day. Advance by short bounds of about 30 yds, with frequent stops for listening. In night operations of this sort it will seldom be possible to attack with covering fire from a flank; actions will be more in the nature of shock action.

STANDING PATROLS

(i) Standing patrols are sent out to watch an approach by which the enemy are expected to advance, usually such places as bridges, road junctions, etc., and give early warning of enemy approach. They may be ordered to change position or withdraw if forced to do so by the enemy.

(ii) The strength of a standing patrol depends on its task, and what resistance it is expected to offer. The strength must be sufficient to provide the requisite number of reliefs for sentry duty.

(iii) The patrol leader must know: –

(a) Points he is to watch or hold.

(b) His route out and back.

(c) What he is to do if enemy appears.

(d) How often to report and by what means.

(e) Any signals he is to give on seeing enemy.

(f) How he is to be recognized on approaching his own lines.

(g) Length of time post to be occupied.

(iv) The patrol is entirely responsible for its own protection, therefore all-round protection is important. Select a position with no covered approaches the enemy may use. Have a good line of withdrawal, and a long field of fire to prevent the enemy getting too close. Scouts to watch both front and flanks. Select a position which is not obvious.

STREET FIGHTING

Street fighting is a slow and exhausting process, the success of which depends on thoroughness. Usually undertaken by small bands of men (sections). When the section leaders have received their orders they make sure they understand them and know what action they are expected to take. They then pass orders on to their men, making sure each man knows his job. Impress on men discipline, no souvenirs. Any questions? Synchronize watches. It is as well to number the section so that if leader becomes a casualty these numbers are the sequence of leadership. Success depends on pushing on, so section cannot stop to attend to casualties. Apply first field dressing and push on coming back to collect later. There are two types of street fighting: –

(a) Concealed street fighting.

(b) Open street fighting.

CONCEALED STREET FIGHTING

(i) Here the enemy have possession of the buildings, and will be concealed in upper floors and on roofs. Tall buildings will be used as look-outs, so always approach under cover of darkness, and after a preliminary reconnaissance surround the town. Each section is given a certain portion of the town, and a rendezvous is established. All instructions are to be given well beforehand, and the best time to attack is at dawn.

(ii) **Weapons**:

Rifle is of little use in street fighting, which is entirely short-range work. Its long barrel makes it a cumbersome weapon.

Grenades, either Mills or home-made, are an important weapon.

Pistol – an important weapon in street fighting.

Sub-machine-gun – best of all weapons for street fighting.

(iii) **Methods**:

Formations depend on circumstances, but as a general rule section divides in two when advancing along the street, half on each side, hugging the buildings. In each half-section there will be one man in front detailed to watch windows and roofs of houses on opposite side of street for enemy. Similarly one man will follow each half-section to deal with anyone opening fire after the section has passed. Remember that back-yards are sometimes a better line of advance than streets.

Action if fired upon from one house: The half-section under fire crosses the street and advances to the house, when both half-sections attack. If both half-sections are fired upon from opposite houses, they both cross the street to the house from which they were fired on, and attack.

Houses to be entered as quickly as possible. A door may be opened by (a) grenade placed at bottom of door; (b) firing sub-machine-gun into lock; (c) ramming the door. If you fail, do not go back the way you came, as enemy will be waiting, but advance. On entering a house the leader quickly details men to various rooms. The enemy is probably on the upper floor, and has an advantage.

Rooms are each attacked by two men. Do not peep round the door, as this is what the enemy is waiting for. One man flings open the door and rushes in, so effecting surprise. The other man waits a moment, then also enters the room. After cleaning out the room, the men report back to their leader. When houses are adjoining it, it is sometimes possible to advance from house to house by blowing holes in dividing walls, and if the room is occupied, throw in a grenade before entering.

Cellars are important places which are difficult to attack. They are best attacked via the stairs rather than the grating. Four men, armed with grenades and pistols, stand at head of stairs and on the signal all jump together, landing with their backs to each other. When the firing starts they may be reinforced. H.E. or smoke grenades are useful in attacking cellars.

(iv) **Reorganization:** After having cleaned out a house, the leader details men to search for weapons, ammunition, and men. Collection of souvenirs is discouraged. He makes central dump of weapons and ammunition, reorganizes, and pushes on.

OPEN STREET FIGHTING

This occurs when the enemy have just taken the town, and have not had time to organize or occupy buildings. Both sides are in the open, and on the same footing. The method of attack is to advance in extended line, shooting during the advance. The main task is to push on, using buildings for covering fire if necessary. Control of the men is essential but difficult under these conditions.

When Defending a House

(i)   Avoid the roof, which may be a death trap and is easily seen from the air.

(ii)   Take all glass out of all windows. Experience has shown that glass splinters cause more casualties than bullets. Barricade windows with sand bags, etc., if there is time, otherwise with mattresses and pillows.

(iii)   A wet blanket hung in front of a window so that it sways gently will stop a bullet.

(iv)   Post sentries where they are protected, and from where they can see both up and down the road. Build a loophole in sandbags.

(v)   Carefully watch both front and back doors.

(vi)   Carry out a reconnaissance and decide on more than one line of withdrawal. Explain these to the men. Retire on the command of the leader only.

(vii)   If explosion occurs and party must quit the house, do not rush out. Make an orderly withdrawal via one of the lines of withdrawal.

(viii) If possible, arrange for all entrances to be covered by fire from some other building.

(ix)   Doors not required should be securely barred and bolted (stout battens, steel rails, etc.).

(x)   Arrange good fields of fire.

(xi)   If possible, place obstacles such as wire close up to foot of exterior walls to prevent the placing of explosive close to walls and also to prevent sudden rushes.

(xii) Illumination at night where possible.

(xiii) Arrange for fire-fighting.

(xiv) Arrange visual signalling, supply of water, S.A.A., etc.

'WE SHALL NOT FAIL OR FALTER'

Winston Churchill

You will have seen that Sir John Dill, our principal military adviser, the Chief of the Imperial General Staff, has warned us all that Hitler may be forced by the strategic, economic and political stresses in Europe, to try to invade these islands in the near future. That is a warning which no one should disregard. [...]

We must all be prepared to meet gas attacks, parachute attacks and glider attacks, with constancy, forethought and practised skill.

I must again emphasize what General Dill has said, and what I pointed out myself last year. In order to win the war Hitler must destroy Great Britain. He may carry havoc into the Balkan States; he may tear great provinces out of Russia; he may march to the Caspian; he may march to the gates of India. All this will avail him nothing. It may spread his curse more widely throughout Europe and Asia, but it will not avert his doom. With every month that passes the many proud and once happy countries he is now holding down by brute force and vile intrigue are learning to hate the Prussian yoke and the Nazi name as nothing has ever been hated so fiercely and so widely among men before. And all the

AFS firefighters in action at scene of enemy bombings, Queen Victoria Street, 1941.

time, masters of the sea and air, the British Empire – nay, in a certain sense, the whole English-speaking world – will be on his track, bearing with them the swords of justice.

The other day, President Roosevelt gave his opponent in the late Presidential Election a letter of introduction to me, and in it he wrote out a verse, in his own handwriting, from Longfellow which, he said, 'applies to you people as it does to us'. Here is the verse:

> …Sail on, O Ship of State!
> Sail on, O Union, strong and great!
> Humanity with all its fears,
> With all the hopes of future years,
> Is hanging breathless on they fate!

What is the answer that I shall give, in your name, to this great man, the thrice-chosen head of a nation of 130,000,000? Here is the answer which I will give to President Roosevelt: Put your confidence in us. Give us your faith and your blessing, and, under Providence, all will be well.

We shall not fail or falter; we shall not weaken or tire. Neither the sudden shock of battle, nor the long-drawn trials of vigilance and exertion will wear us down. Give us the tools, and we will finish the job.

9 February 1941

'A VERY LARGE FIRE WAS IN PROGRESS'

Commander Sir Aylmer Firebrace

The next serious raid deserving of mention occurred on the night of 16–17 April 1941. It lasted for eight hours – the enemy sending over four hundred and fifty bombers. This raid produced the highest total of fires that ever occurred in the London Region in one night. Of these 1,500 were in the L.C.C. area, including 400 which were classified as 'serious', that is to say, requiring more than ten pumps to extinguish them.

Once more St Paul's suffered damage, being hit by a 500-lb. H.E. bomb, as well as by a heavy shower of incendiaries. Here I would like to express my admiration for the stout-hearted local defenders of St Paul's. Without their constant watch and ward, the cathedral – a most difficult building to safeguard – must have been destroyed. The Prime Minister, Mr Churchill, was solicitous for the safety of the building, and on 9 September 1940, the LFB received an urgent message from him, asking that special attention be paid to saving St Paul's – a fire in Old Change was threatening the safety of the building.

Again the resources of the Region were severely strained, and 120 pumps came in from other Regions to lend a hand. On this night a large number of parachute mines were dropped, no less than eleven falling in Westminster alone.

I happened to learn that a senior L.F.B. officer had recorded his experiences during this raid. Yielding to my request he sent it to me; it gives a vivid picture of the life of a fire officer (and of his firewoman driver) during the blitz.

On the evening of the 16 April 1941, the sirens sounded early, and I stood by in fire kit in the District Control awaiting the receipt of calls. Shortly after the raid started, one was received to the BBC in Portland Place. I at once ordered my car and went on. On arrival the officer in charge reported to me that he had made it a ten-pump fire. A very large bomb had devastated the rear of the main building of the BBC, also involving the annexe. About a dozen buildings were well alight, and the fire was spreading. I took over control, made it a thirty-pump fire and requested two turntable ladders.

Upon the arrival of the Chief Superintendent I turned over to him, and, taking a party of men, I commenced a search of the rear part of the building, which had taken the full impact of the bomb and blast. Where once had stood a series of two, three, and four-storied buildings was now only a heap of rubble. During the progress of the fire, other small fires, caused by flying embers, broke out on surrounding roofs, and it was necessary to keep the turntable ladders constantly on the move in order to attack them.

During the course of operations, there was a sudden change in the direction of the wind, and I noticed the branchman at the top of one of the ladders suddenly become enveloped in flame. Instructions were immediately given for him to be brought down, and he was taken to my car where

my firewoman driver rendered first aid. The injured man was badly burned about the face, and later removed to the Middlesex Hospital.

Branches were now in position and the fire was well surrounded.

❊   ❊   ❊

Upon my return to the District Control at Manchester Square for further instructions I was informed that a sub-station in the Chelsea area had received a direct hit, one fireman being killed, several injured, and one still missing. I immediately proceeded to this incident. Whilst on my way, when turning out of Grosvenor Square, with my despatch rider following close behind me, a stick of three bombs came whistling down. One struck a building 100 yds in our rear, and in a flash the dispatch rider shot past the car at about sixty miles per hour. The next bomb dropped in front of us, and in the flash of the burst I could see the coping stones leaving the building as we were passing. The third bomb of the stick dropped ahead of us in Hyde Park, near the gun sites. When we turned into Park Lane, I signalled the dispatch rider to stop, and upon inquiring why he had increased his speed and passed us, he stated that it had not been of his own volition, but was caused by the blast of the exploding bomb.

When I arrived at the sub-station in Chelsea, I found that a large bomb had demolished a corner block of flats and had severely blasted the station. The dead fireman had been removed and the injured were receiving attention from a first-aid party. The missing man had not been located, so, after making some inquiries, I commenced a personal search of the area. About 200 yds from the station, I found a steel helmet, and, lying face downwards in the gutter about 20 yds from the spot, under coping stones and debris, I found the missing man. There was no doubt that he was dead.

I then went back to the sub-station to ascertain the condition of the remainder of the staff. The firewomen were still carrying out their jobs efficiently, but the control room was thick with dust; they were in a filthy condition and obviously badly shaken. Arrangements were therefore made with the local station at Brompton Road for them to be relieved; owing to the blasted condition of the station and the fact that the water and gas services were out of action, it was impossible for them to get a hot drink or anything to eat.

I then went to Brompton Fire Station in order to get in touch with the District Control. I was told to proceed to Ebury Street, Pimlico, and take charge of a fire zone. Upon my arrival I found a furniture depository well alight. A district officer was in charge, and he reported that he had made it a twenty-pump fire; it was well surrounded and no further help was required. I then went to Imperial Airways, a sub-station on Westminster's ground, where I linked up with the Chief Superintendent, and we both proceeded to a fire area in Sutherland Street, Pimlico. Here we found a scene of devastation extending over a large area. Several fire appliances had been hit and there were ambulances and other vehicles very severely damaged. It transpired that an H.E. bomb had dropped earlier in the evening, setting light to surrounding buildings, and that, about ten minutes prior to our arrival at the scene, the same area had been hit by a parachute mine.

Here we saw an amazing, and, despite the conditions, amusing sight – an area of devastation, a very large crater in the road practically filled with water, a gas main alight and blazing furiously, the whole area lit by fires; and there, sitting in his shirt sleeves on the edge of the crater, his feet dangling in the water, was an auxiliary fireman, calmly cleaning out the strainers of two trailer pumps; he thought they had been choked by débris from the crater. He appeared to be completely oblivious of everything around him – the fires, the gunfire, and the falling bombs. Choked strainers we discovered, however, were not the cause of the trouble, but water turbulence caused by the rush of water in the crater. We assisted him to remove his suctions to another part of the crater, and within a few minutes he was able to start his pumps and supply water to the firemen waiting on the branches.

On the way back, and proceeding towards Buckingham Palace, we observed several flares dropping and lighting up the neighbourhood. Upon reaching the foot of Constitution Hill we turned round as we estimated that it would not be long before something dropped. Whilst passing the front of Buckingham Palace, we were looking through the rear windows of the car when, in the distance, we saw two very vivid orange flashes, from which it was apparent that two large fires had broken out somewhere in the Victoria Street area. Passing through Buckingham Gate we shortly afterwards discovered Christ Church, Broadway, alight from end to end. We could also see another fire in progress in Petty France. The Chief Superintendent proceeded to Petty France and left me in charge of the Church. Very soon afterwards a trailer pump arrived and I ordered the officer in charge to make the pumps up to six and to ask for a turntable ladder.

THE STIRRUP HAND PUMP

I then made my way towards Petty France where the roof of a ten-storied building was well alight. Two trailer pumps had arrived and were setting into the nearest hydrants. The men proceeded to tackle the fire with great determination and had it under control in under an hour, confining it to the top floor and roof.

Arriving back in Broadway, I found that a turntable ladder had arrived, and, as the fire had gained a good hold on the roof, the driver was instructed to pitch his ladders and endeavour to save the eastern end. The Chief Superintendent and I again joined forces and we made our way to Westminster Fire Station on foot. Whilst going back to the Station, a shower of incendiaries fell in the Horseferry Road area, but most of them burnt themselves out in the street and in the playground of the Greycoat School.

Upon arrival at Westminster we were very thankful to get a cup of tea. We were then told that Brompton Fire Station had received a direct hit by parachute mine and that several persons were missing. We immediately ordered the car. Whilst walking through the appliance room towards the door, a stick of bombs fell in the vicinity, blasting the appliance doors open, but we didn't wait to see the results of this.

On reaching the Brompton locality, we found the approaches to the station blocked with débris, and had to proceed on foot. The station had not received a direct hit but a large bomb had fallen immediately opposite in Chelsea Square, and it was reported to us that eight firemen were buried in the débris. It was made a ten-pump fire, and certain of the personnel were used to dig and search for their missing comrades. Three men, severely injured, were recovered after a time, but all died later.

After leaving this incident we learned that, very soon after we had left Christ Church, Westminster, a bomb had dropped on the turntable ladder which had been at work, injuring several firemen. We proceeded there at once. On our arrival we found that a pump had been severely damaged by an H.E. bomb and also that an oil bomb had struck the base of the turntable ladder, setting fire to it and to another appliance alongside. The officer in charge of the fire reported that one fireman had been killed and seven badly injured. He also informed us of a very remarkable incident. When the turntable ladder had been struck by the bomb, its upper extension had fallen forward onto the blazing church, the branchman at the top being knocked unconscious by the impact. With the seriousness of the position on the ground, the man at the top of the ladder had been overlooked. However, some time later, he regained consciousness, and, without any assistance, unhooked himself and made his way to the ground. Apart from shock and abrasions he was otherwise unharmed and carried on at the fire. The final casualties from this fire were: one killed outright; two subsequently died of their injuries; two lost limbs, and three others severely injured. After ensuring that all the injured men had been removed to hospital, and that the fire was extinguished, we made our way to Westminster Fire Station to ascertain the general fire position in the district. We learned that Selfridge's in Oxford Street had received a direct hit and had been made a fifty-pump fire.

The Superintendent of 'A' District (North) was in charge on our arrival, and he informed us that there was a shortage of water. A plan of campaign was decided upon, and a relay was put into operation, using the dry pipe line from the

Serpentine to Marble Arch, and thence by lines of hose into dams erected in Oxford Street.

At this point the Chief Superintendent received a message to say that the Marylebone Goods Yard at Lisson Grove had been hit and a very large fire was in progress; the pumps had been made up to one hundred. The Chief Superintendent immediately gave me instructions to take over the fire, and he and the Divisional Officer 'A' (North) went on to the Goods Yard.

Several pumps had by this time reported to me and these were immediately utilized to attack the fire on the top floor.

❊   ❊   ❊

The fire was eventually under control at 09.00 hours in the morning. I left the building at about 09.30 to proceed home to Manchester Square for a hot bath and some breakfast. But this was by no means the finish of the day, either for my firewoman driver or myself; by 10.15 we were out again making a tour of all the fires in the West End, including those in the Westminster area and the one at Selfridge's, in order to ascertain that all fires were receiving attention, that the crews were being relieved for meals, and that fresh crews were dealing with the work of turning over.

We eventually completed the tour of fires at 13.30 hours. […] I then went off to bed for a few hours sleep in order to be ready for the night.

'WE SHALL COME THROUGH'

Winston Churchill

… In some quarters of the House, or at any rate among some Members, there is a very acute realization of the gravity of our problems and of our dangers. I have never underrated them. I feel we are fighting for life and survival from day to day and from hour to hour. But, believe me, Herr Hitler has his problems, too, and if we only remain united and strive our utmost to increase our exertions, and work like one great family, standing together and helping each other, as 5,000,000 families in Britain are doing today under the fire of the enemy, I cannot conceive how anyone can doubt that victory will crown the good cause we serve. Government and Parliament alike have to be worthy of the undaunted and unconquerable people who give us their trust and who give their country their all.

It is a year almost to a day since, in the crash of the disastrous Battle of France, His Majesty's present Administration was formed. Men of all parties, duly authorized by their parties, joined hands together to fight this business to the end. That was a dark hour, and little did we know what storms and perils lay before us, and little did Herr Hitler know, when in June, 1940, he received the total capitulation of France and when he expected to be master

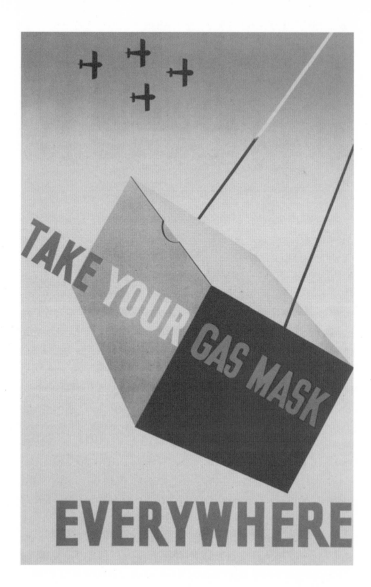

of all Europe in a few weeks and the world in a few years, that 10 months later, in May, 1941, he would be appealing to the much-tried German people to prepare themselves for the war of 1942. When I look back on the perils which have been overcome, upon the great mountain waves in which the gallant ship has driven, when I remember all that has gone wrong, and remember also all that has gone right, I feel sure we have no need to fear the tempest. Let it roar, and let it rage. We shall come through.

7 May 1941

ATTACK ON WESTMINSTER

General Raymond E. Lee

I t was a lovely, calm, silvery, coolish Sunday morning, with not many people out early. What wrung my withers and made me feel extremely angry was to see a large hole burned in the roof of Westminster Hall, which was built by William Rufus and is the only remaining part of Westminster Palace. The House of Commons is completely burned out by fire, so it will be a long time before Winston Churchill can stand pounding the despatch box in front of the Government bench, under the eye of the bewigged Speaker in his ancient chair. The Deanery in the yard of Westminster Abbey is completely wrecked by fire and a long tangle of hoses was running into the Abbey itself, where the lantern, just over the spot where the King and Queen were crowned, had been burned through. Some damage had also been done to the stonework of the Henry VII Chapel, but this is not irreparable. A much more modern structure, Thames House, on the Embankment, had had a large bomb on the top corner, and the huge blocks of stone which fell from the cornice were scattered thickly over the Embankment road and the side streets. One had landed on top of a taxi and completely demolished it.

I lunched alone and afterwards walked around a little bit more. Park Lane is blocked, with a huge crater in the middle of it, not far

A Shelter in Camden Town under a Brewery, Christmas Eve, 1940 by Olga Lehmann.

from Lord Londonderry's house. Part of Shepherd's Market is completely burned out, together with a large building across the street, and a number of the mansions in Hill Street are simply brick shells still smoldering. In Clarges Street there is a house down. As we passed it this morning, we saw the Salvage Corps digging furiously through a heap of rubbish to rescue some unfortunate who was buried beneath it. When I walked by there this afternoon, they were still digging but rather more slowly and it is easy to see that the ambulance which was standing there awaiting the removal of the bodies is now going to take only corpses.

11 May 1941

HOME SECURITY
WAR ROOM DIARY
11 MAY 1941

REGION NO.5

The following is a *selection* of messages received in Home Security War Room from London Region only during three hours of the attack on London of 11 May 1941.

Time of origin	Form of message	In or out	Subject	Message No.
0036	Teleprinter	In	SOUTHWARK. H.E. Borough Road blocked. Mains damaged. WESTMINSTER 0004. H.E. Dolphin Square. No cas. LAMBETH 2325. H.E. Norwood Road blocked. BETHNAL GREEN 2350. H.E. Roman Road. Mains dam. ISLINGTON 2342. Heavy incendiary attack. H.E. at Stonefield Road. ST MARYLEBONE 2340. H.E. Wells Street. ST PANCRAS 2350. H.E. H.E. at HARROW and I.B.s at CAMBERWELL, TWICKENHAM, FELTHAM and HAMMERSMITH.	13
0040	"	"	POPLAR 2358. East India Dock No. 12. Half dock on fire.	14
0045	"	"	POPLAR 2359. South West India Dock Office wrecked by H.E.	15
0050	"	"	POPLAR 2359. Cootes Barge Road to right of S.W. India Dock entrance. 12 barges alight.	17

0055	"	"	STEPNEY 0020. Part of No. 9 warehouse boundary wall opposite No. 8 St Catherine Dock destroyed by H.E.	18
0055	"	"	WESTMINSTER. H.E. approx. 0027. Westminster Cathedral. Further details not yet available.	19
0102	"	"	HOLBORN report fire at British Museum, Gt Russell Street. No further details yet.	22
0116	"	"	CITY 0005. I.B.s on P.L.A. H.Q. Trinity Square. Fires extinguished. BETHNAL GREEN 2350. I.B.s Fires. HAMMERSMITH 0018. 3 H.E. 20 casualties, including 18 trapped. WANDSWORTH 0015. 3 H.E. Wardens Post damaged. Casualties. LAMBETH 0005. H.E. 6 casualties. 0014. H.E. Westminster Bridge Road blocked. Bombing at CROYDON, BERMONDSEY, BARNET.	28
0145	"	"	WEST HAM 2350. No. 25–27 Sheds, Royal Albert Dock fired by incendiaries. Fairly extensive damage to export goods.	38
0158	"	"	SOUTHWARK. H.E. River wall bank, side near power station; river wall damaged. Tide now rising. Possibility of flooding.	46
0200	"	"	WESTMINSTER 0024. I.B. Children's Hospital, Vincent Sq., Fire.	47
0230	"	"	WESTMINSTER 0155. 3 H.E. Chambers of Houses of Parliament.	59
0232	"	"	ST PANCRAS 0010. 3 H.E. Charlotte St area. 10 casualties. ISLINGTON 0037. 10 H.E. across borough. Property and mains dam. Many casualties. L.M.S. Railway Bridge at Corsica St dam. and in dangerous condition. No report of effect on Railway traffic yet.	61
0241	"	"	POPLAR 0055. P.L.A. report H.E. on mine-sweeper H.M.S. *Goatfell*. Believed direct hit.	64

0247	"	"	POPLAR 0115. P.L.A. report owing to damage to impounding station, S.W. India Dock, all power including high tension off.	67
0244	Telephone Fire Control	"	20-Pump fire at Railway Goods Yard, Silverthorne Road, Clapham, WANDSWORTH. 60-Pump fire at Westminster Hall, WESTMINSTER.	70
0300	Teleprinter	"	BERMONDSEY from 2358 onwards. Heavy attack by H.E. and I.B.s especially in Rotherhithe area. Much damage to dwelling houses and business premises. Casualties unknown. CHISLEHURST 0106. H.E. Valliers Wood Road, casualties trapped. WESTMINSTER 0017. H.E. Bruton Street. Casualties. WANDSWORTH 0057–0123. 6 H.E. and many I.B.s Damage to dwelling houses, flats and church. Casualties.	81
0325	"	"	H.M.S. *Tower* lying Cherry Garden Pier, BERMONDSEY, has received direct hit. Many casualties.	88
0326	"	"	ST PANCRAS. H.E. 0255. De Gaulle's Headquarters, Gordon St, 10 casualties, some trapped. Headquarters partly demolished.	89
0334	"	"	ST MARYLEBONE 0040. 3 H.E. Fire and damage. ST PANCRAS 0035. 13 H.E. Widespread damage. At least 60 casualties. PADDINGTON 0055. 2 H.E. Casualties trapped. LAMBETH 0040. 3 H.E. 18 casualties. Considerable damage.	93

NIGHT AFTER NIGHT AFTER NIGHT

MAJOR NIGHT BOMB ATTACKS ON UK CITIES AND TOWNS, 7 SEPTEMBER 1940–16 MAY 1941

Target Area	Number of Major Attacks	Tonnages of H.E. Aimed
London	71	18,291
Liverpool-Birkenhead	8	1,957
Birmingham	8	1,852
Glasgow-Clydeside	5	1,329
Plymouth-Devonport	8	1,228
Bristol-Avonmouth	6	919
Coventry	2	818
Portsmouth	3	687
Southampton	4	647
Hull	3	593
Manchester	3	578
Belfast	2	440
Sheffield	1	355
Newcastle-Tyneside	1	152
Nottingham	1	137
Cardiff	1	115

OFFICIAL INSTRUCTIONS ISSUED BY THE MINISTRY OF HOME SECURITY

GAS ATTACK

HOW TO PUT ON YOUR GAS MASK

Always keep your gas mask with you – day and night. Learn to put it on quickly. Practise wearing it.

1. Hold your breath. 2. Hold mask in front of face, with thumbs inside straps.
3. Thrust chin well forward into mask, pull straps over head as far as they will go.
4. Run finger round face-piece taking care head-straps are not twisted.

IF THE GAS RATTLES SOUND

1. Hold your breath. Put on mask wherever you are. Close window.

2. If out of doors, take off hat, put on your mask. Turn up collar.

3. Put on gloves or keep hands in pockets. Take cover in nearest building.

IF YOU GET GASSED

BY VAPOUR GAS Keep your gas mask on even if you feel discomfort
If discomfort continues go to First Aid Post

BY LIQUID or BLISTER GAS

1	2	3	4
Dab, but *don't rub* the splash with handkerchief. Then destroy handkerchief.	Rub No. 2 Ointment well into place. *(Buy a 6d. jar now from any chemist).* In emergency chemists supply Bleach Cream free.	If you can't get Ointment or Cream within 5 minutes wash place with soap and warm water	Take off at once any garment splashed with gas.

PRINTED FOR H.M. STATIONERY OFFICE BY ROW & CROW LTD., LONDON (91306)

'WHEN THEY SOUND THE LAST ALL CLEAR'

Louis Elton

When they sound the last all-clear
How happy, my darling, we'll be
When they turn up the lights
And the dark lonely nights
Are only a memory.

Never more we'll be apart
Always together, sweetheart
For the peace-bells will ring
And the whole world will sing
When they sound the last all-clear.

We've got our troubles and we've got our cares
But as long as we keep smiling through
There'll come a day
When the clouds roll away
And the sun will be shining anew.

When they sound the last all-clear
How happy, my darling, we'll be

An ARP warden plays the piano during a sing-a-long in an air raid shelter in November 1940.

When they turn up the lights
And the dark lonely nights
Are only a memory.

Never more we'll be apart
Always together, sweetheart
For the peace-bells will ring
And the whole world will sing
When they sound the last all-clear.

SOURCES AND ACKNOWLEDGEMENTS

Evelyn August, 'Hands Across the Black-out', from *The Black-out Book* (Osprey Publishing, 2009), by permission of Leonora Dossett.

Alice Bridges, Birmingham, 'If there is a bomb with your name on it …', from Dorothy Sheridan (ed.), *Wartime Women: A Mass Observation Anthology* (Mandarin, 1991), pp.93–5. Reproduced with permission of Curtis Brown Group Ltd, London on behalf of the Trustees of the Mass Observation Archive. Copyright © The Trustees of the Mass Observation Archive.

Vera Brittain, 'London's Hour', September 1940, and 'Bombed but still carrying on', November 1940, from *England's Hour* (Macmillan & Co, 1941), pp.195–8; 261–5. Extracts from Vera Brittain's *England's Hour* are reprinted by permission of Mark Bostridge and Timothy Brittain-Catlin, Literary Executors for the Vera Brittain Estate 1970.

Herbert Brush, 'One enormous hole', 26 October 1940, from Sandra Koa Wing (ed.), *Our Longest Days: A People's History of the Second World War* (Profile Books, 2007), pp.51–2. Reproduced with permission of Curtis Brown Group Ltd, London on behalf of the Trustees of the Mass Observation Archive. Copyright © The Trustees of the Mass Observation Archive.

M.E. Chifney and G.A. Hollingsworth, 'Coventry, 14 November 1940', from the Private Papers of M.E. Chifney, IWM 3793, Department of Documents at the Imperial War Museum; Diary from the Private Papers of G.A. Hollingsworth, IWM 4391, Department of Documents

David Heneker, 'The Thingummy-Bob', words and music by Barbara Gordon, David Heneker and Basil Thomas © 1941, reproduced by permission of Francis Day & Hunter Ltd, London W8 5SW.

A.P. Herbert, 'Goering … Goering … Gone' and 'Last Words', from *Let us be Glum* (Methuen & Co., 1941), by permission of A.P. Watt Ltd on behalf of M.T. Perkins, Polly M.V.R. Perkins and The Executors of the Estate of Jocelyn Herbert.

'How to Wear Your Gas Mask' from *Air Raid Precautions: An Album to contain a series of Cigarette Cards of National Importance* (W.D. & H.O. Wills/Home Office, 1939), pp.11–13. By permission of Imperial Tobacco UK.

F.W. Hurd, 'East End Ablaze', from the Private Papers of F.W. Hurd, IWM 4833, Department of Documents at the Imperial War Museum. Every effort has been made to trace the copyright holder in Mr Hurd's papers, but this has not been possible. The publisher and the Imperial War Museum would be grateful for any information which might help to do so.

General Raymond E. Lee, 'Attack on Westminster', from *The London Journal of General Raymond E. Lee, 1940–1941* by Raymond E. Lee, pp.272–3, Copyright ©1971 by Jeanette Baker Lee. By permission of Little, Brown & Company.

Doris Melling, 'The Biggest and Best air raid ever', Liverpool, 30 August 1940, from Sandra Koa Wing (ed.), *Our Longest Days: A People's History of the Second World War* (Profile Books, 2007), pp.42–4. Reproduced with permission of Curtis Brown Group Ltd, London on behalf of the Trustees of the Mass Observation Archive. Copyright © The Trustees of the Mass Observation Archive.

James A. Milne, 'Fitness for Liberty!', from *Fitness in Defence: a manual of physical training and P.T. tables specially devised for the Home Guard, National Fire Service, Air Raid Wardens, War Reserve Constabulary, Air Training Corps, the Boy Scouts, the workers, the people* (Link House, London, 1940), pp.5–7.

Harold Nicolson, 'The Bombardment Continues', from diary entries in Harold Nicolson, *Diaries and Letters 1930–1964* (Penguin, 1984), pp.192–4; 201. Reproduced with permission from the Harold Nicolson Estate.

Mollie Panter-Downes, 'Bad Nights, Worse Nights and Better Nights', 14 and 21 September 1940, from *London War Notes, 1939–1945*, edited by William Shawn (Longman, 1972), by permission of Lady Baer.

E.A. Platt, 'Everything seemed to be burning', from the Private Papers of E.A. Platt, IWM 6958, Department of Documents at the Imperial War Museum, by permission of Mrs M.H. Platt.

J.B. Priestley, 'London's Defiant Spirit', 15 September 1940, from J.B. Priestley, *Postscripts* (William Heinemann, 1940), pp.72–5. Excerpt by J.B. Priestley from *Postscripts* (© J.B. Priestley, 1940) is reproduced by permission of PFD (www.pfd.co.uk) on behalf of The Estate of J.B. Priestley.

John Strachey, 'The Ton Bomb', from John Strachey, *Post D: some experiences of an air-raid warden* (Gollancz, London, 1941), pp.76–97. By permission of Charles Strachey.

Joan Wilshin, 'We could see little puffs of smoke', from the Private Papers of K.J. Wilshin, IWM 14408, Department of Documents at the Imperial War Museum, by permission of Professor Sue Macmillan.

'Your Refuge-Room', from *The Protection of Your Home against Air Raids* (1938), pp. 8–10; 'Rendering Your Refuge-Room Gas Proof' from *Air Raid Precautions: An Album to contain a series of Cigarette Cards of National Importance* (W.D. & H.O. Wills/Home Office, 1939), pp.3–4. By permission of Imperial Tobacco UK.

The compiler and publishers are grateful to the above for permission to include extracts. While every effort has been made to contact copyright holders, in a few cases this has proved impossible. If, in these cases, the copyright holders contact the publisher, we will be pleased to include an acknowledgement in any future editions.

Other sources are:

The 'Fourth Defence Service', 'All hands to the Pump' 'Taking Shelter', from *Air-Raid Precautions Training Manual No. 1: Basic Training in Air Raid Precautions* (1940), pp.6–10; 13–20; 29–31.

'Things to do in an Air-Raid', from *The Protection of Your Home against Air Raids* (1938), pp.22–8.

'Air Raid Precautions for Animals', from *Air Raid Precautions Handbook No. 12: Air Raid Precautions for Animals* (1939), pp.2–6; 10.

'Home Security War Room Diary, 11 May 1941' and 'Night after Night after Night: Major Night Bomb Attacks on UK Cities and Towns, 7 September 1940–16 May 1941', from T.H. O'Brien, *History of the Second World War: Civil Defence* (HMSO, 1955), pp.681; 688–9.

'Manning the Home Guard', 'Halt, Advance, Deploy' and 'Encountering the Enemy', from *Home Guard Manual* (1941), pp.9–12; 25–7; 172–6; 192–5.

'Showers of sparks and burning embers', from *Fire over London 1940–41* (London County Council, 1941), pp.30–2.

The following books have also been useful:

Arthur, Nigel, *Swansea at War* (Archive Publications, 1988)

Calder, Angus, *The Myth of the Blitz* (Jonathan Cape, 1991)

Calder, Angus, *The People's War: Britain 1939–1945* (Pimlico, 1992)

Fire over London 1940–41 (The London County Council/Hutchinson, 1941)

Ray, John, *Night Blitz 1940–1941* (Cassell, 1996)

The compiler would also like to express her gratitude to the following: the staff of Cirencester and the Bodleian Libraries; the Archivists at the Imperial War Museum for their help and the Trustees of the Imperial War Museum for allowing access to papers in the Department of Documents; my mother, Christine Mitchell, for sharing her memories with me; and everyone at Osprey, most particularly Jon Jackson, Kate Moore and Emily Holmes.

ILLUSTRATIONS

Illustrations of cigarette cards on pp. 39; 40; 41; 65; 99; 100; 101; 110; 119; 131; 185; plate section p.3 by permission of Imperial Tobacco UK.

The publisher is grateful for permission to reproduce wartime images and posters from the following:

Imperial War Museum: p.14 IWM HU 672; p.17 IWM H 2646; p.20 IWM PST 13850; p.29 IWM PST 13889; p.34 IWM PST 3751; p.47 IWM H 3499; p.56 IWM D 4355; p.79 IWM H 8111; p.83 IWM PST 13871; p.89 IWM D 4568; p.95 IWM PST 00753; p.97 IWM D 1680; p.103 IWM PST 13891; p.107 IWM HU 1129; p.128 IWM PST 13869; p.135 IWM D 1631; p.139 IWM D 2618; p.155 IWM H 5598; p.158 IWM D4117; p.161 IMW Q (HS) 99; p.163 IWM: PST 14817; p.190 IWM PST 13860; p.193 IWM ART LD 13860; p.196 IWM PST 0142; p.199 IWM PST 00136; p.201 IWM D 1564; plate section p.1 IWM PST 14849; plate section p.7 IWM PST 1497; plate section p.8 IWM HU 659

London Fire Brigade: p.87; p.151; p.177

Mary Evans Picture Library: plate section p.4; plate section p.5

Mirrorpix: p.49 WA1993071

National Archives: p.113 Inf-3-400; p.147 ZPER 34193; plate section p.6

Science and Society Picture Library: p.62 Photo Manchester Daily Express; p.91 National Railway Museum; plate section p.2 National Media Museum; plate section p.8 National Media Museum